The Open University

A Second Level Course

STUDY GUIDE 3
ISSUES IN WOMEN'S STUDIES

Prepared for the Course Team by
Gill Kirkup with Barbara Hodgson

THE OPEN UNIVERSITY U207 *ISSUES IN WOMEN'S STUDIES* COURSE PRODUCTION TEAM

Amanda Willett, Barbara Hodgson, Catherine King (Chair), Diana Gittins, Dinah Birch, Felicity Edholm, Fiona Harris, Frances Bonner, Gill Kirkup, Harry Dodd, Helen Crowley, Joan Mason, Judy Lown, Kathryn Woodward, Laurie Smith Keller, Linda Janes, Linda McDowell, Lizbeth Goodman, Maggie Riley, Maureen Adams, Meg Sheffield, Melanie Bayley, Randhir Auluck, Richard Allen, Rosemary Pringle, Siân Lewis, Susan Crosbie, Susan Himmelweit, Susan Khin Zaw, Tony Coulson, Veronica Beechey, Wendy Webster

External Assessor: Elizabeth Wilson, Professor of Policy Studies, Polytechnic of North London

The Open University
Walton Hall
Milton Keynes MK7 6AB

First published 1992

Copyright © 1992 The Open University

All rights reserved. No part of this publication may be reproduced, stored in a retrieval system, or transmitted, in any form or by any means, without written permission from the publisher or a licence from the Copyright Licensing Agency Limited. Details of such licences (for reprographic reproduction) may be obtained from the Copyright Licensing Agency Ltd of 33–34 Alfred Place, London WC1E 7DP.

Designed by the Graphic Design Group of The Open University

Printed in the United Kingdom by the Open University

ISBN 0 7492 0104 5

This publication forms part of the Open University course *U207 Issues in Women's Studies*. If you have not enrolled on the course and would like to buy this and other Open University material, please write to Open University Educational Enterprises Ltd, 12 Cofferidge Close, Stony Stratford, Milton Keynes MK11 1BY, United Kingdom. If you wish to enquire about enrolling as an Open University student, please write to the Central Enquiry Office, The Open University, P.O. Box 200, Walton Hall, Milton Keynes MK7 2YZ, United Kingdom.

1.1

Cover illustration by Christine Tacq

3918C/u207sg3i1.1

CONTENTS

	Introduction	5
	Aims	6
	Timetabling	7
1	**The nature of science and technology (Week 15)**	10
1.1	Introducing science and technology	10
1.2	What are science and technology?	15
	Article 1.1 'Discovering and doing ...' by Laurie Smith Keller	15
1.3	Beginning a feminist critique of science	17
	Article 1.2 'Women's voices, men's voices: technology as language' by Margaret Lowe Benston	18
1.4	Developing a feminist critique of science	19
	Article 1.3 'How gender matters ...' by Evelyn Fox Keller	20
	Article 1.4 'How the women's movement benefits science: two views' by Sandra Harding	20
	Introduction to Book One, *Knowing Women*	21
2	**Our bodies, our minds, our selves (Weeks 16–17)**	22
2.1	Introduction	22
2.2	What is the nature and importance of biological sex differences?	23
	Article 2.1 'In pursuit of difference' by Lynda Birke	26
	Thinking about empirical evidence	28
	Summary: feminism and the biological bases of gender	29
2.3	Origins, anthropology and feminism	29
	Article 2.2 'The changing role of women in models of human evolution' by Linda Marie Fedigan	30
2.4	Medicine: a masculine science	33
	Defining and identifying health	35
	Article 2.3 'Women and medicalization: a new perspective' by Catherine Kohler Riessman	36
2.5	Reproduction: control, contraception and abortion	42
	The concept of reproductive rights	44
	Article 2.4 'Detecting genetic diseases ...' by Lynda Birke, Susan Himmelweit and Gail Vines	45
3	**Women producing science and technology (Weeks 17–19)**	47
3.1	Introduction	47
3.2	Women practising science	48
	From the top	48
	Opposition and difference	48
	Using scientific biography	51

3.3	**Women scientists in the making?**	55
	Article 3.2 'Girls in science education …' by Liz Whitelegg	57
	Why do girls need science education?	60
3.4	**Women in engineering**	61
3.5	**Technology, production and power**	62
	Article 3.4 'Technology, production and power' by Cynthia Cockburn	62
3.6	**The technology of warfare**	65
	Article 3.6 'A brother in arms, a sister in peace …' by Julie Wheelwright	67
3.7	**Technology and women's work in underdeveloped countries**	68
	Article 3.7 'Science, technology and development' by Radha Chakravarthy	68
3.8	**Conclusion**	70
4	**Consuming science and technology (Weeks 19–20)**	71
4.1	**Technology, science and houses**	71
4.2	**Science, technology and housework**	80
	Article 4.1 'Domestic technology: labour-saving or enslaving?' by Judy Wajcman	82
4.3	**Domestic technology in ecological and economic crisis**	86
	Article 4.2 'Cold hearths and barren slopes …' by Bina Agarwal	87
	Health risks	90
4.4	**Consumption and information technology**	90
	Article 4.4 'The social construction of computers …' by Gill Kirkup	92
4.5	**Ecofeminism**	93
5	**Conclusion: science, technology and imagining the future**	96
	Answers to Activities	98
	Objectives	101
	References	102
	Acknowledgements	103

INTRODUCTION

Women's studies was originally concerned with two particular aspects of science and technology: the exclusion of women from the professions of science and technology and countering biologically determinist theories about gender. However, during the 1980s feminist work on science and technology increased and became more systemic, so that the connections between a number of diverse aspects became better understood, and they can now be brought together in a course like this as a coherent area of study.

We have been selective in the issues we have chosen for this part of the course. We believe that you need to understand some of the theoretical debates about the nature of science and technology and about whether such things as feminist science and technology are either possible or desirable. These debates are presented in the first week of work on Book Three, *Inventing Women*, and although they are not simple debates you will find that they are no more difficult than some of the theoretical material you have already coped with earlier in the course. You will also find that these questions are implicit in the case-study material in Chapters 3 and 4. By looking at actual issues and events you can test whether you find the theoretical debates in the first chapter insightful ways of understanding women's interaction with science and technology that help inform our strategies for action. However, in women's studies, as well as in science, a theory is not rejected because it cannot explain *everything* you are interested in; instead it is held up to scrutiny for modification and eventual displacement by a better theory – if and when one is developed.

In the second chapter of Book Three you will look at what biology and anthropology have had to say about sex difference and gender behaviour, and how the practice of medicine, which draws on these disciplines, has conceptualized women, our bodies and their functions. Chapters 3 and 4 look at how science and technology structure women's lives both in paid employment and in the domestic environment.

However, as well as content there are methods which are part of science (and social science) and technology; these are tools which enable you to explore the material world and to test your theories about it. In this Study Guide there are some simple statistical exercises which ask you to read and critically assess tables and graphs and also exercises to help you to think critically about the way in which experiments are carried out and technical innovations are evaluated. This is an important aspect of 'literacy' in the 1990s, and is especially important for anyone wanting to adopt a critical feminist position on issues in science and technology.

AIMS

There are common themes through all the parts of the course and it is worth reminding you of those which are particularly significant in this one: sex and gender, difference, social constructionism and essentialism, language and representation, equality, power, and the public and the private. You may also find it useful to look back at Section 3 of the Course Guide to remind yourself of the overall course aims. The work in Book Three and this Study Guide contributes to all of these, as well as having the following specific aims:

1. To show how the areas of knowledge and expertise called 'science' and 'technology' have defined women and helped to construct a gendered world.

2. To examine critically the impact of selected scientific and technological applications on the lives of different women in the 1980s and 1990s, both as producers and consumers and be aware of differences due to race, class and country.

3. To review a range of feminist positions on science and technology, and examine the idea of a feminist science and technology and what it might mean.

4. To develop the skills to evaluate statistical data presented in tables and graphs, and be aware of the limitations of the experimental method.

At the end of this Study Guide you will find a detailed list of the objectives, that is the specific things which we hope that we have taught you by the time you have completed your work on Book Three and this Study Guide. You will find it a useful list to help you review your work then, and as a revision aid near exam time.

TIMETABLING

We are aware that at this point in your study of U207 you are having to reconcile a number of demands. Summer School is approaching, you will be working seriously on your project; and, although you have just had a review week, you may be slightly behind in your study of the material. Don't worry too much about this last event; in our experience it is very common for this to happen to OU students at this point in the year, whatever the course. But because of this we have produced a map of the work for Book Three and related material, to show how we feel it would be best distributed over over the six weeks allocated to it. Rather than a rigid plan for you to follow we offer this as a guide: do adapt it to your own circumstances.

► **ACTIVITY 1** ◄

Spend about twenty minutes looking at the plan and reading our comments about it below. Then modify it until it reflects your own situation: scribble over it putting in those personal things which will also place demands on you during these weeks, for example school and family holidays, preparing for Summer School. Spending these few minutes now might save you time and panic later!

1. The four sections of the Study Guide and Book Three do not divide equally between the six weeks that you have to study them. Chapter 2 and Chapter 4, we estimate, will take you longer than a week each. For Chapter 2 this is because you will have to spend most of your time on extensive and in some cases more difficult texts, while for Chapter 4 the texts are very accessible but you will find a number of lengthy activities associated with them in this Study Guide.

2. Although the TMA timetable changes slightly each year we expect that you will have to submit a TMA at the end of your final week of study of this part of the course. The TMA question will presume that you have completed your work on Book Three, so that you must schedule time for writing your TMA after you have completed your study of the texts. You may need to spend six to eight hours on your TMA, so we suggest that you schedule in that time during Week 20.

3. We are also aware that at the same time as you begin the first week's work on Book Three you will probably have a TMA based on Book Two work for submission, and we suggest you take this into account in planning your personal schedule for this work.

4. Television and radio programmes for this book do not have a one-to-one relationship with chapters or articles. They tend to have a thematic connection. However, we have indicated those programmes which have the most direct connection with material here, some of which will have been broadcast well before you began work on Book Three. If you missed them at the time of broadcast please make sure that you see them either at Summer School or at your study centre. Again, time to watch and listen and to make notes on relevant programmes should be counted into your study schedule.

5. At this stage in the course you should be beginning to do serious work on your project. Some of the activities in this Study Guide have been designed to help you think about your information collection, and about the way you might want to present the biography of your subject. We expect that during the time you are working on Book Three you will be

Study Plan for Book Three, *Inventing Women*, and related material

Week No.	Readings from Book Three	Special Study Activities	Associated Media *(In italics where they relate to Book Three but are not in chronological sequence)*	Assessment	Project Associated Work	Connections to other Books	Important Personal Events
15	Chapter 1 Intro A1.1 Smith Keller A1.2 Benston A1.3 Fox Keller A1.4 Harding	Data analysis of students		(TMA04: you will probably be handing in this TMA during this study week. Associated with work on Study Guide 2)	Project outline submission with TMA 04	Book One Introduction	
16	Chapter 2 Intro A2.1 Birke A2.2 Fedigan	Analysis of Sex Discrimination Act clauses	Radio 06 Transsexualism *Radio 03 No Sacred Bond (Wk 7)*			Book One A2.1, A2.2	
17	*Chapter 2 ctd* A2.3 Riessman A2.4 Birke, Himmelweit and Vines Chapter 3 Intro 3.1 Mason 3.3 Kirkup and Keller	Personal Workbook to reflect on your experience of medicine? Thinking about biographies	*Radio 02 Mothers and Daughters (Wk 4)* *TV 02 The Body Social (Wk 5)*			Study Guide 1A – anorexia	
18	*Chapter 3 ctd* 3.2 Whitelegg 3.4 Cockburn 3.5 Piercy		*TV 06 Designing production (Wk 21)*		Planning the focus of your biography and thinking about its syle and your explicit role	Book Two/Study Guide 2, A4.1, A5.1, A5.5	
19	*Chapter 3 ctd* 3.6 Wheelwright 3.7 Chakravarthy Chapter 4 Intro 4.1 Wajcman 4.2 Agarwal 4.3 Breeze	Matrix reading and house design Domestic technology	Radio 07 Women and the military *TV 04 Public Space; Public Works (Wk 13) and TV 06 (Wk 21)*			Book Two, A4.1, A4.5	
20	*Chapter 4 ctd* 4.4 Kirkup 4.5 Cox 4.6 Hossain		*Radio 04 Religious Rebellions (Wk 10)*	(TMA 05 will probably fall due next week and be associated with Study Guide 3 and Book Three)			

putting aside significant time at least to plan your project. Ideally you should also make a significant start on collecting what you need (see the Biographical Project Book). This too needs planning into your schedule, so that when you attend Summer School, where you will spend significant amounts of time on activities associated with the project, you will have already made a start on your own project.

1
THE NATURE OF SCIENCE AND TECHNOLOGY
(WEEK 15)

1.1 INTRODUCING SCIENCE AND TECHNOLOGY

What comes to your mind with the word 'science'? Images of white-coated men (or women?) working through the night on the solutions to problems that will change the world? Einstein working on his theory of relativity? Alexander Fleming finding penicillin in mould growth? Oppenheimer's team at Los Alamos developing a nuclear bomb? Marie Curie in her shed discovering uranium? Perhaps you also associate it with memories of your school science lab with its pervasive smell of gas and chemicals, where you carried out nervous experiments with Bunsen burners and could never produce the observations that your teacher expected of you.

In our culture science is endowed with almost unlimited power – to solve the problems of the planet, or to destroy all life. Scientists are credited with authority often way beyond any expertise they possess. They can like David Bellamy become media personalities because they are insightful about issues and they can communicate well. However, others are often insensitive to the limits of their expertise and authority and their access to published journals and other media gives them a forum to present personal opinions as though they were scientific theories. An example of this is the chemistry professor who in 1991 used his position as editor of a physics journal to publish unpopular and unfounded arguments about the effect of working mothers on students' behaviour (see Figure 1).

Phrases like 'advanced technology' or 'scientifically tested', and esoteric scientific words have been used so widely, especially in advertising, that we now regard them with suspicion. There is now a reaction to this and a whole new language of 'green' advertising based on notions of the 'pure' and the 'natural' is taking their place. The West in the twentieth century has become suspicious of science. If we look at a painting like Mary Cassatt's 1893 picture 'Young women plucking the fruits of knowledge and science' (Plate 6 in Book Three and part of a mural which is reproduced here in full: see Figure 2), we see a Victorian optimism about the benefits of science which would be hard to find today amongst women who are not scientists themselves.

Feminist critiques of science and technology are part of a movement to re-assess these activities, their aims and their methods. However, before you begin to study these critiques, we feel that it is important that you spend some time examining what science and technology are in the modern world. You may be one of that small number of people who have studied science, or technology, or who work in these areas, but from what we know about the background of students who take women's studies courses, this is unlikely to be the case.

Cheat slur costs job

FROM **JOHN DRISCOLL**
PETERBOROUGH

AN ARTICLE in the prestigious Canadian *Journal of Physics* blaming working mothers for the abberant behaviour of today's youth, has sparked a furore among academics, led to a front page apology and the resignation of the publication's editor.

The article was submitted by Gordon Freeman, University of Alberta chemistry professor, who was guest editor of the special edition last December, and reported his personal observations that students were cheating more than they had when he began teaching in 1958.

Based on informal discussions with his students for more than 30 years, Mr Freeman concluded that "about 50 per cent of students whose mothers worked outside the home had a strong tendency to cheat" on examinations.

He went on to argue that this cheating was part of a larger pattern of aberrant behaviour that included embezzlement, infidelity, political and business corruption, drug use, teenage sex and "the murder of 14 female engineering students at L'École Polytechnique in Montreal".

Dozens of complaints arrived at the publishers, the National Research Council. Readers were upset with both the conclusions and the lack of solid data or any evidence of formal scientific research.

Figure 1
Source: *Times Higher Education Supplement*, 6 September 1991

Figure 2
'Modern Woman', Mary Cassatt's decoration of the South Tympanum of Woman's Building, World's Columbian Exposition, 1893 (building and painting destroyed)

► **ACTIVITY 2** ◄

Table 1a–c gives you data about a one-year intake of undergraduate students (omitting Associate students) who took the women's studies course that predated this one. Look at the data and then answer the questions below.

Table 1a Students on the women's studies course by sex

Sex	No.	As % of total
Male	27	7
Female	381	93

Table 1b Students on the women's studies course by occupation

Occupation on entry	No.	As % of total
Housewives – full-time	90	22
– part-time	43	11
Armed forces	2	0
Administrative and managerial	14	3
Teachers – primary	20	5
– secondary	18	4
– higher education	7	2
– other	2	0
Medical professions	34	8
Social services	16	4
Other professions and arts	21	5
Qualified science and engineering	3	1
Technical personnel	10	2
Skilled trades	1	0
Other manual work	2	0
Communications and transport	3	1
Clerical and office	65	16
Sales and services	21	5
Retired	29	7
In institutions	7	2

Table 1c Previous foundation courses taken

	No.	As % of total
D102	212	52
A102	145	35
A101	99	24
T101	21	5
M101	18	4
D101	16	4
S101	11	3
A100	9	2
D100	5	1

(a) What percentage of the students that year were men?

(b) Which is the largest occupational category amongst this group of students?

(c) Which is the largest occupational category of paid work?

(d) Discounting medicine, what are the percentages of students in scientific or technical jobs?

(e) What is the ratio of students working in science and technology to those working in clerical and office jobs?

(f) Can you see any problems with interpreting the data as they are presently categorized?

(g) Finally, look at Table 1c showing the previous foundation courses of this group. What has been the most popular faculty for students to have studied a foundation course in and which the least popular?

Answers to these questions will be found at the end of the Study Guide.

▶ ACTIVITY 3 ◀

The occupations of OU women's studies students are not unusual. Look at the bar charts in Figure 3. These charts represent the numbers of students studying four major academic areas at UK universities during 1985-86 (at that time polytechnics were not included in these figures).

Use Figure 3a–d to answer the following questions:

(a) Which subject of study has the largest numbers of women, and which the smallest?

(b) Which subject of study has the largest number of men and which the smallest?

(c) Compare the numbers of women studying pure science at all levels and the numbers studying applied science.

(d) What are the total number of women in first degree courses in the four areas, and the total number of men?

(e) What proportion of the total number of men in first degree courses are studying applied science and what proportion of women?

(f) What proportion of the total number of men studying in each area at first degree level go on to study postgraduate courses and how does this compare with women?

Answers to these questions will be found at the end of the Study Guide.

COMMENT

You cannot give an accurate answer to question (f) based on the data you have, because the postgraduate students in the charts are different people from the undergraduates and we cannot know exactly how many of those 1985–86 undergraduates will in their turn go on to postgraduate study. However, you can compare the numbers you have been given as proportions. In doing this you will have seen that in every area a smaller proportion of women go on to postgraduate study than men; this is even the case where women are in the majority at undergraduate level. You were probably surprised to see that in what is considered a 'female' subject – Arts – nearly twice the proportion of men went on to postgraduate work as did women. The numbers of women studying applied science is very small, and pure science, which includes maths, is probably higher than you expected.

Discussion of the causes of the behaviour that these figures represent will come in section 3 of this Study Guide. First we think that it is important to establish some conceptual groundwork about the nature of modern science and technology, and for you to begin your study of Book Three, *Inventing Women*.

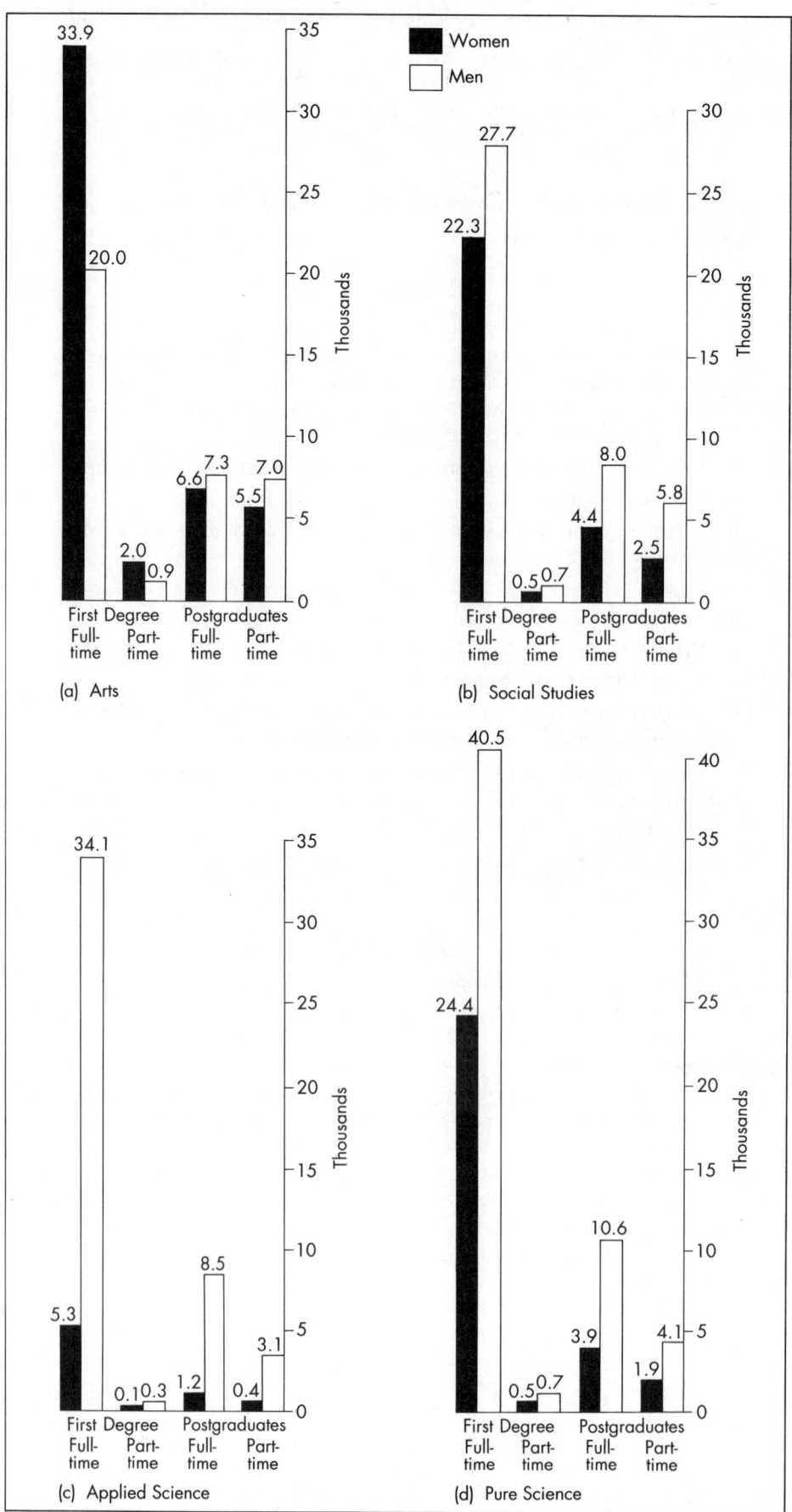

Figure 3
University students by sex and mode of attendance, 1985–86, United Kingdom
Source: EOC, 1988

1.2 WHAT ARE SCIENCE AND TECHNOLOGY?

Article 1.1 'Discovering and doing ...' by Laurie Smith Keller

Turn to Article 1.1, 'Discovering and doing: science and technology, an introduction' by Laurie Smith Keller. Smith Keller describes at its very beginning the two purposes she has in writing the article. Make a note of these and when you have finished reading, decide how well you think she has fulfilled them. You may need to give the article more than one reading because it encompasses a wide range of issues and topics.

▶ **ACTIVITY 4** ◀

It may help you to make notes on the following concepts. If you are still puzzled by the meaning of some of them when you have read the article a couple of times, do as Smith Keller suggests: try looking in a dictionary, and also discussing them with other students.

Science – what is it and what is the basic assumption that underlies it?

What is objectivity and what do you understand by the notion of the separation of the subject and the object? You might like to relate the ideas presented here with some of the material you have already studied about subjectivity in Book One.

What is meant by 'holistic' views of nature, and who do you associate with these views?

Define and describe the experimental approach to science.

Describe 'value-free' science.

Compare big science and little science.

What are reductionism and a mechanistic view of the world? Contrast these with 'holism'.

What is an hypothesis, and think of some examples of your own?

Smith Keller presents three models of technology. What are they and can you describe the differences between them?

What do you understand by intermediate or alternative technology?

COMMENT

Smith Keller describes science as a human intellectual and social activity whereby we try to make sense of phenomena and predict them. It presumes that the material world is measurable and consistent so that it is possible to generalize about phenomena. Modern science entails a set of techniques which presume that it is possible to separate the subject (observer) from the object of study, and so produce 'absolute' data about its form and behaviour. This position, she argues, has been criticized from within modern physics for what it presumes about the material world, as well as from within psychology and social science for its model of human perception and consciousness.

A 'holistic' view is not the only alternative model to a mechanistic (machine-like) view or reductionist view (where complicated phenomena are explained by reference to some 'essential' feature), but holistic views have been popular in the 1980s, especially those concerned with ecology, in particular the Gaia hypothesis.

The notion of 'value-free' science – that science is simply an intellectual method or tool equally available to be used for good or evil – is criticized by most of the authors in this course. One of the main planks of feminist theory has been that the pre-feminist theories about the world reflected a male-dominated culture and the values embedded in it, and pure science is affected by this inherent bias as much as any other activity.

An hypothesis is a statement about a causal connection that is made in order to be tested. It is considered the starting-point for most scientific research. A simple example of an hypothesis is 'women have better physical endurance than men'. This stays as an hypothesis until I collect data about the endurance of women and men and compare them to see whether they support this idea or not. If the data do, the hypothesis is 'accepted'. It is not a theory. A theory would propose a reason or cause as to why this is the case, and it would be built by testing a number of hypotheses, for example that female hormones contribute to endurance, or the experience of childcare, or childhood socialization. It is the explanatory theory that is of most interest to any scientist; the hypothesis is only a means to build the theory.

There are many ways in which we encounter science and the claims made for it in our daily lives. Consequently we need to be able to judge for ourselves what, or how much, to believe and what actions to take as a result of information or claims. Such information is made public in a variety of ways in the press and other media, in political decision-making areas, over dinner tables – often for a very particular purpose – and it is a useful skill to be able to interpret data and to ask questions about not only what is there but what is *not* there.

► **ACTIVITY 5** ◄

In this activity we are asking you to be critical about an attempt to verify 'scientifically' an apparently scientific claim. Look again at Smith Keller's discussion of scientific methods and then read the following fictionalized account of an experiment.

Good Bye Fat: a slimming aid that really works

A few years ago a so-called wonder drug was being advertised with the claim that 'you can eat as much as you like; this new drug will cause pounds to be shed'. This drug was apparently a 'starch blocker' which interfered with the enzyme amalyse, a substance in the body normally responsible for the breakdown of starch. Some users claimed the drug worked wonders, others found their excess weight as hard to shift as it had always been.

An evening newspaper decided to check out these claims and invited its readers to assess 'scientifically' the value of this drug. Six volunteers were selected, their initial weight recorded and then measured over the experimental period of one month. Table 2 summarizes the findings.

Table 2

Name	Initial Weight	Final Weight	Comments
Sue	9st 4lbs	8st 10lbs	'absolutely delighted'
Ingmar	14st 7lbs	13st 0lbs	'completely useless'
Nazir	8st 6lbs	8st 5lbs	'pleased to lose some weight'
Norman	13st 11lbs	13st 14lbs	'very disappointed'
Jane	10st 6lbs	–	'gave up'
Rebecca	9st 2lbs	8st 13lbs	'forgot to take some pills'

In its report, the newspaper made much of Sue's delight, implying the successful demonstration of a 'slimming aid that really works'.

What conclusions do you feel should properly be drawn from this experiment?

The report didn't mention that Sue ate normally over the month of the trial but that she gave up alcohol during that period and that Ingmar started playing squash towards the end of the month's trial. If it had, would your conclusions have been different?

Do you have any reservations about the newspaper's scientific methods? How well does it correspond with Smith Keller's description of the process?

What other information would you have liked to have before accepting or rejecting the newspaper's implied conclusion? How would you plan a similar experiment?

COMMENT

I hope you agree that no general conclusions could be drawn at all! Four out of six people apparently lost weight but we have no information about the conditions under which this happened – except that apparently most of them took some of the pills.

Even with the additional information about Sue and Ingmar, no general conclusions are warranted. What that information alerts us to is that there was no attempt to standardize treatment during that month. Sue gave up alcohol and Ingmar took up squash and their weight loss may have been caused by abstinence or activity, rather than by starch blockers. And we can't be sure that some or all of those who lost weight were not already doing so before the experiment began.

From the information given we can hardly even guess at the experimental design. Replicating (that is, repeating exactly) the experiment from this account would be impossible. The independent variable is the taking of pills and the dependent variable is the change in weight. The experimental conditions are, of necessity, limited to a prescribed dosage of pills but different time periods might have been considered – a second month perhaps. There was no mention of a control (that is, matched – in age/weight/sex) group of people who did not take the pills. The sample of volunteers is small and heterogeneous, neither random nor chosen from a defined population. We are given no idea what steps were taken, if any, in the experimental design to minimize or negate effects of variables (such as increased exercise) other than the independent variables; such variables are known as confounding variables for obvious reasons.

The important aspects of designing an experiment of this kind are to obtain a sound sample and to devise a suitable control. The sample needs to be as large as possible. Individuals differ in their initial weight and in their response to a trial of this type. Thus in a very small sample, one or two atypical individuals will seriously distort the overall picture. The greater the number of individuals, the more likely a general picture will emerge, particularly if the participants are approximately homogeneous with regard to initial weight, alcohol and exercise habits etc. and of the same sex. A control for this kind of experiment is likely to be of the 'double-blind' variety. Instead of having an equivalent group not taking pills, everyone will take pills but some will be taking the starch blockers and others a placebo (that is a pill which looks the same but has no active effect). The double-blind is that the experimenter administering the pills to the group her/himself doesn't know which are which either, in order to minimize unconscious interactive effects between the experimenter and the group.

1.3 BEGINNING A FEMINIST CRITIQUE OF SCIENCE

Turn now to the Introduction to Chapter 1. Read as far as the paragraph beginning 'Evelyn Fox Keller – the author of Article 1.3 ...' (pp. 5–8) and stop there.

THE NATURE OF SCIENCE AND TECHNOLOGY

The articles in Chapter 1 are dealing with a philosophical area called *epistemology*, which is concerned with how we know things. Much epistemology concerns itself with science since modern science has been proposed as *the* method which will produce true knowledge of the world. But epistemology is also about how you or I know something to be true from our own perceptions and memories. Feminist scholars in the 1970s and '80s have produced critiques of research methods across a variety of academic areas, social science and history being some of the earliest and science and maths being some of the more recent.

You should distinguish epistemology from *ontology* which is concerned with questions about whether things exist. Most epistemology presumes that they do, and is concerned with how we know about them.

Three important theorists are mentioned in this part of the introduction:

- Thomas Kuhn (born 1922), whose book *The Structure of Scientific Revolutions* (1962) has had long-term influence in the history of science. His book is written in an accessible style, and although there are many critics of his ideas, they remain especially important to feminists because they can be used to explain why modern science is so patriarchal.

- Michel Foucault (1926–1984), a French philosopher and historian interested in the history of ideas. You have already met his work earlier in the course and will study it more deeply in the following weeks.

- The pages you have just read also introduce you to the writings of Evelyn Fox Keller. She has been one of the most significant feminist writers on science in the 1980s, and you will notice that apart from the article by her which is included in the book, many of the other authors refer to her work and quote her.

Article 1.2 'Women's voices, men's voices: technology as language' by Margaret Lowe Benston

Article 1.2 by Margaret Lowe Benston is written in a clear, almost polemical style and it introduces some of the ideas that will be taken up more extensively through *Inventing Women*.

> Key concepts
> technique
> experts (men as) and expertise
> power (a key course concept) and how technology is implicated in it

Now read Article 1.2. While you are doing so, make notes about the following.

How does Benston see the world views of men and of women differing?

She introduces the work of Carol Gilligan, whose book *In a Different Voice* (1982) has become very important for a variety of areas of feminism, and especially in women's education. Make notes of what Benston says about Gilligan's work. You will find yourself returning to her ideas at a number of points in your work on Book Three.

Explain in your own words Benston's notion of technology as a language of social action and give examples.

Explain in your own words her notion of technology as self-expression, again giving examples.

The article is mainly about how women are disadvantaged by their lack of access to technology but Benston argues that this also has implications for men; what are these?

Benston's discussion of technology as a language of social action may be a bit confusing at first. You will be looking at language later in the course and this will help you to decide whether you think Benston's analogy is a useful one. She is saying that *men* generate meaning through language and that language then structures social interaction. However, meaning is generated through perception and experience and men's experience of the world is different from women's. Men experience a technological world. The problem is that perception must be mediated through language which means that Benston appears to be setting up a closed loop in which it is impossible to identify the direction of a causal relationship, or the best point to make an intervention. Not an unusual tangle to get into in a philosophical or political discussion.

A simplified version of Gilligan's argument is that men's world view is concerned with cause and effect, order, control and rationality, and women's with emotion, commitment, responsibility towards others and resolution of conflict.

► **ACTIVITY 6** ◄

Look at Benston's personal anecdotes early on in her article, and the way in which she now sees them as a part of a social process. This would be a good point for you to try and recall your own experiences of technology and science during a similar, probably crucial, period of your adolescence. Use your Personal Workbook first simply to jot down your memories about how you felt during your teens about such things as school science lessons, cars, bikes and other machines, and electronic gadgets such as radios.

Can you identify any events which you now see as demonstrating cultural expectations, to which you did or did not succumb?

1.4 DEVELOPING A FEMINIST CRITIQUE OF SCIENCE

Return now to complete your reading of the Introduction to Chapter 1 (pp. 8–10). As you read, make notes on the following as they will help you when you come to read the actual articles by Evelyn Fox Keller and Sandra Harding.

What are the questions Fox Keller identifies about women and science?

What do you understand by dualism (a concept you should already be familiar with)?

What do you understand by relativism?

What is empiricism?

What, if anything, do you know about post-modernism?

Fox Keller identifies the following questions about women and science:
- What is wrong with women that we can't do science?
- If science is gender-neutral and there is nothing wrong with women, what are the social barriers that keep women out?
- If science is inherently masculine, what would a women's (or feminist) science be?
- How has gender shaped the construction of science, and science gender?

Fox Keller believes that dualism is implicit in much of our thinking, including feminist thinking, and it limits our capacity to create good science. She thinks that discussion of a feminist science also reflects dualist thinking.

Sandra Harding, whom you will also meet again when you come to study the last chapter of *Knowing Women* (Article 8.1), is concerned with two kinds of feminist positions: empiricism and standpoint theory. Empiricism is the use of methods/ideas based on practical experience rather than theory. Harding identifies empiricists as criticizing the social practices of science but not science itself, whereas standpoint theorists criticize science as an activity which they see as permeated by gender, class and race.

Post-modernism or post-modern feminism has been touched on briefly in Book One and the early chapters of Book Two. For our purposes here it is enough that you see it as an even more relativist position than that of the standpoint theorists.

Article 1.3 'How gender matters, or, why it's so hard for us to count past two' by Evelyn Fox Keller

Fox Keller's article is very rich. You are unlikely to follow the subtleties of her arguments with only one reading. We therefore suggest that you read it through once quickly to obtain an overview, underlining or using a highlighting pen to mark important concepts and arguments. Then read it through a second time more slowly making notes.

> Now read Article 1.3. The following will help you to focus the notes you make on your second reading.
>
> What does Fox Keller mean by the 'one-two step' and the 'two-one step'?
>
> She argues that it seems very difficult for human beings to think outside either a universalistic notion of science or a dualistic one. Are you clear about what she means by this?
>
> She accuses proponents of 'feminist' science of having similar dualistic thinking to patriarchal society: do you understand her argument? Keep her criticism in mind and decide as you proceed through the book whether you agree with her.
>
> She argues that it is important to get past 'dualistic' thinking and think in terms of difference. Difference is a major theme in the course, and one you have already explored extensively. Here we see it operating in the field of science – its language, its method and its social context.
>
> You will be studying part of Fox Keller's biography of McClintock in Chapter 3. She has been used as an important exemplar, demonstrating how modern science could be different *and* produce important new theories.
>
> What does Fox Keller mean by the capacity to count between one and two, and why are women more likely to have this capacity? Can you relate this to any of the psychoanalytical theories you met in Book One?
>
> She argues that it is very hard for women to be scientists without experiencing inauthenticity or alienation. Why is this the case?
>
> The final part of her article is about the debate between theories of competition and co-operation in evolutionary discourse. At first glance this is not a debate about the way science is gendered – unlike the debate that you will study in the next chapter between 'Man the Hunter' and 'Woman the Gatherer' where gender is explicit. But Fox Keller is arguing that the debate between competition and co-operation is based implicitly on equally strong romantic notions about masculinity and femininity, reflecting an unreal but very strong duality.

Article 1.4 'How the women's movement benefits science: two views' by Sandra Harding

Sandra Harding's article moves away from a focus on what constitutes science to an examination of different feminist positions as bases for action and intervention. This is the first of two articles by her in the course. The second which you will study later in the course elaborates some of the ideas here but for a different audience. Article 1.4 was first published in *Women's Studies International Forum* in 1989. Harding has written extensively on feminism and the philosophy of science; her book *The Science Question in Feminism* (1986) is a very scholarly analysis of many of the issues being dealt with throughout Book Three.

Turn to Article 1.4. Again you might like to read this article through twice. It will help you to pull out the important points if you make notes on the following as you read.

In her first paragraph she lays out the problem she is addressing. What is it? *what exactly does the woman's movement contribute to the growth of knowledge.*

She sees one of the main differences between feminist critics of science to be that some think that only some science is 'bad' and it can be made 'good', whilst others think that all science as it is presently carried out is 'bad'. Which group do you sympathize with most? (You can always change your mind later!) *bad!*

List the problems faced by feminists who adopt a radical critique of *all* science? *how much to be involved? — where to start? how ..?*

What are the problems faced by those who only criticize *some* science? *selecting.*

What is the goal that she identifies as the one all feminist critics of science should be moving towards? *working against traditionalists.*

What do you understand as 'positivist' science?

Summarize what you think Harding means by feminist empiricism. What can be achieved by feminist empiricism in science and what are its disadvantages?

What is meant by standpoint theory and what are its achievements and disadvantages?

Harding concludes by trying to be even-handed in her criticism of both positions and ends up arguing for a very pragmatic position which says both activities are useful in the feminist project of remaking science. The suggestion is that we must use the tools we have at hand for the job.

These critiques of science are implicit in much of what you will be reading in the rest of the book. You will find it useful as you read to ask yourself: along a continuum of critical positions (rather than a duality!), where would you place the author, or the activity described?

Introduction to Book One, *Knowing Women*

▶ **ACTIVITY 7** ◀

Your final activity for the first week of study on Book Three is one that links what you have been studying here with your work on Book One and the work on post-modernism which follows.

Re-read the Introduction to *Knowing Women*. Do not spend a long time on this: the most relevant part is the first long section. It reminds you that feminist critiques of science are part of a larger feminist critique of knowledge. It also elaborates more than we have done here on post-modernist critiques of knowledge.

You are now ready, we hope, to dive more deeply into some particular areas of science, to find out how they are gendered and how feminism is addressing that gendering.

2
OUR BODIES, OUR MINDS, OUR SELVES (WEEKS 16–17)

2.1 INTRODUCTION

Your work in the next week and a half will deal with some of those aspects of science and technology that theorize our bodies, and out of which techniques and social structures are developed. We continue the debate opened in Book One, Chapter 2. There are only four articles in Chapter 2 of Book Three but we estimate that, in order to study them to the kind of depth we recommend, you will need to spend about a week and a half. Check your own pace against the recommended timetable at the beginning of this Study Guide.

In this chapter we will also be discussing the nature of empirical data in biological and anthropological theory and beginning a critical consideration of statistics. But this does not mean that we deny the value of subjective experience especially with regard to our bodies, which, as Lisel Mueller writes, is where we live:

> The light
> drains me of what I might be,
> a man's dream
> of heat and softness;
> or a painter's
> – breasts cosy pigeons,
> arms gently curved
> by a temperate noon.
>
> I am
> blue veins, a scar,
> a patch of lavender cells,
> used thighs and shoulders;
> my calves
> are as scant as my cheeks,
> my hips won't plump
> small, shimmering pillows:
>
> but this body
> is home, my childhood
> is buried here, my sleep
> rises and sets inside,
> desire
> crested and wore itself thin
> between these bones –
> I live here.
> (Lisel Mueller, 'A Nude by Edward Hopper')

2.2 WHAT IS THE NATURE AND IMPORTANCE OF BIOLOGICAL SEX DIFFERENCES?

Regardless of what feminists have argued about the social construction of gender there is a firmly held, commonsense belief that biological sex difference is important enough to merit different treatment in law, and to serve as an explanation of gendered behaviour. Even the UK Sex Discrimination Act has a clause about instances where discrimination in employment in favour of one sex is legal if sex is a 'genuine occupational qualification' (GOQ).

▶ **ACTIVITY 8** ◀

(a) Can you think of any employment situation where you think that biological sex *would* constitute a genuine occupational qualification?

(b) Now read the following three examples of actual GOQs and identify for each the implicit assumptions made about gender difference.

> S7(2)(a) Where the essential nature of the job calls for a man (or woman) for reasons of physiology (excluding physical strength or stamina) – an example might be modelling clothes – or in dramatic performances or other entertainment for reasons of authenticity, so that in either case the essential nature of the job would be materially different if carried out by a person of the other sex.
>
> S7(2)(b) Where considerations of decency or privacy require the job to be held by a man (or woman), either because it is likely to involve physical contact between the jobholder and men (or women) in circumstances where they might reasonably object to the jobholder being of the opposite sex or because the jobholder is likely to work in the presence of people who are in a state of undress or are using sanitary facilities and who might reasonably object to the presence of a person of the opposite sex to themselves. It might be claimed, for example, that being a man was a GOQ by virtue of this provision for a job as a men's changing-room attendant.
>
> S7(2)(f) Where the job needs to be held by a man because of restrictions imposed by the laws regulating the employment of women. Factories legislation, for example, limits the times at which women may work in certain places. It may therefore be necessary to an employer to restrict to men certain jobs involving night work.

(Home Office, 1975)

COMMENT

(a) You probably came up with a short but varied list, including perhaps priests, sumo wrestlers or swimwear models. I had a problem. There are many situations when I would prefer a job to be done for me by one particular sex. But preference is not a genuine occupational qualification. Could you put your preferences to one side?

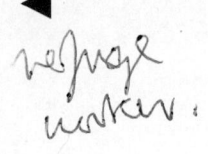

(b) None of these paragraphs refers to differences in reproductive function or reproductive biology, but they each make presumptions about the relationship between other aspects of biological sex and some other attribute. For example S7(2)(a) is about people who have the visual characteristics of one sex, rather than any other measure. Male-to-female transsexuals have been very successful 'female' models: see Figure 4. Example S7(2)(b) confuses sex with sexuality – that people are all heterosexual, and that contact between men and women in particular situations is either sexual or indecent or both. You may have found clause S7(2)(f) a curious inclusion because it says little except that if previous 'protective' employment legislation restricted women's working this restriction continues to be legal. We have included it here because protective employment legislation originally conceived of women (and children) as significantly weaker physically and therefore restricted their employment in particular heavy and dangerous jobs; the most well-known example is that of coal-mining.

Figure 4
Caroline Cossy, a male to female transsexual and a very successful 'female' model, arriving at the European Court for Human Rights in 1990, in an attempt to gain the right to marry as a woman

Despite the fact that Clause S7(2)(a) specifically excludes physical strength or stamina from grounds for GOQ, a later clause in the Act makes a specific case for continued sex discrimination in sport on those very grounds.

> S44 There is a general exception for acts relating to participation as a competitor in certain sporting events which are confined to one sex. The sports to which the exception applies are those in which physical strength, stamina or physique are important, so that the average woman would be at a disadvantage in competition with the average man.
>
> *(Home Office, 1975)*

This clause continues to protect exclusively male areas of sport against mixed-sex competition, some of which – for example children's team games or adult snooker – appear to have little to do with strength, stamina or physique and do not apply in other countries.

Are the widely held beliefs about sex differences in strength, stamina or physique based in fact? Women's sporting records have been improving faster than men's but have not yet equalled men's for the same events. How much is this due to biologically based difference, or different socialization and training, or the use of various drugs to overproduce certain 'masculine' characteristics even in men? Answers to these questions are not only relevant to campaigns around access to sport, but will also influence social ideology implicit in legislation.

Figure 5
Sculpture of muscular female athlete from Sparta (530 BC) where women could be strong without eliciting derogatory remarks

▶ ACTIVITY 9 ◀

In your study of Book One *Knowing Women,* you were introduced to debates about the relevance of biological arguments to discussions of gender difference. Note down here, as a reminder for yourself, brief definitions of:

gender role *The role female or male you have been brought up to be.*

gender identity *the gender you identify with*

social constructionism *how society trains you to behave as either male or female.*

biological determinism *how your sexual characteristics dictate what you are*

> If you need to remind yourself of any of these terms look at Study Guide 1A and your own notes for Chapter 2 of *Knowing Women*, 'Biology and society'. Also remind yourself of Lynda Birke's arguments about the nature of the relationship between biology and society. Skim-read again her article 'Transforming biology' from Book One for the answers to the following questions:
>
> What are the ways in which feminist arguments challenge biological determinist arguments about sex and gender?
>
> Why is it important *not* to deny the importance of our bodies?

COMMENT

Biological determinism is challenged:

(a) through questioning the scientific evidence which is used to justify it, and which often turns out to be poor evidence or open to alternative interpretations;

(b) emphasizing the importance of social effects;

(c) questioning the automatic dichotomies implied by male/female, biology/society, mind/body terms;

(d) questioning the universal notions explicit in discussions of the biology of a race or species.

Birke argues that social constructionist arguments have over-emphasized the social and, through denying the importance of the body, have reinforced the Cartesian[1] idea of a mind/body separation. This then leads to blind spots in feminism over such things as genetics, the relationship between human beings and animals, the ways in which biology and society interact to transform each other. This transformative relationship is very similar to the dialectical relationship discussed by Alison Jaggar in Article 2.2 in Book One.

Article 2.1 'In pursuit of difference' by Lynda Birke

In Book Three there is another article by Lynda Birke – 'In pursuit of difference: scientific studies of men and women'. This looks in detail at what is known about physiological sex difference, in order to answer the questions: what is the nature of the empirical evidence about biological sex difference, and what does it mean?

> Turn to Article 2.1 now and read the first three sections only and the box entitled 'Chromosomes, genes and inheritance' (pp. 81–90). Make notes on the following:
>
> • the difference between chromosomes and genes
>
> • the influence of dominant and recessive genes on inheritance
>
> • the influence of chromosomes on foetal development.
>
> Look up a definition of 'hormone'.
>
> Look carefully at Figure 2.1.3. What does this figure indicate about male development?
>
> What is the difference between androgens and progestins, and why should you be careful of the term 'male hormone'?
>
> Figure 2.1.4 is a graph illustrating muscle development in boys and girls. At what age are boys' and girls' muscles almost equivalent, and

---

[1] 'Cartesian' is the description given of any philosophical position similar to that of the philosopher René Descartes (1596–1650). He believed that the body and the mind or soul were distinctly different things although connected whilst the body was alive. The body was seen as almost mechanical, and animals, who had no souls, were almost equivalent to automata. The body and its functions could be explained by science, the soul not.

at what age do they diverge dramatically? If you wanted to scrutinize the data on which this graph was drawn, what would you need to know?

Figure 2.1.5 illustrates some basic physiological differences between adult men and women. Summarize them for yourself.

Summarize for yourself the sex-related physiological changes that occur with old age.

Birke argues that there are physiological differences between males and females at all stages of development, from the foetus to old age, but that these differences are not *absolute* even at the chromosomal level. This means that individuals from either sex can exhibit many characteristics of the other sex. It is also why you should beware of the term 'male hormone' since it describes the 'masculinizing' effect of a hormone which is in fact produced by *both* men and women.

When you are presented with figures such as 2.1.3, 2.1.4 and 2.1.5, ideally you need to know details about the population from which the data came, such as how many individuals there were, whether they were from the same racial groups, cultures, classes or geographical locations. All this affects how far you can accept the figure as a representation of something universal. Muscle development, for example, is highly related to nutrition, and this will depend on income, resources and whether there is differential food allocation between boys and girls.

Now read the first four paragraphs of 'What is a "difference"?' (pp. 90–92), stopping at the paragraph beginning 'A third problem with ...', and examine Figure 2.1.6 in detail.

Graphical representations like those in Birke's article are very useful to those of us who are not mathematically inclined since they give us a visual image of the data in a way which makes more sense intuitively than a mathematical description such as the mean and standard deviation. However, graphical representations can be misleading and should always be scrutinized.

In Figure 2.1.6 Birke is simply demonstrating that, given any individual's height, it would be very difficult to tell what sex they were unless they were a small woman or a tall man, since the overlap between men and women with respect to their heights is very large.

Read the rest of this section (pp. 92–5), making notes on the following.

What is the effect of the exercise and activity on physical differences between men and women?

What do you understand by 'metabolic rate'?

What is osteoporosis, and how is it caused? Is it always more prevalent in women than men?

Look carefully at Figure 2.1.7. In what ways is this kind of graphical representation open to criticism?

Physiological characteristics are affected by a variety of factors such as age and exercise; therefore the characteristics of both groups and individuals change over time. Even when the empirical data shows a sex-related physiological difference, it is not always clear how this difference relates to the capacity to do certain activities. It is interesting that female characteristics have usually been interpreted as causes of weakness.

We also want to draw your attention to the interpretation of Figure 2.1.7. This is a pictogram, where data are represented by a symbol rather than a line or bar, and the relative size of the symbols indicates the relative differences between the data represented. Figure 2.1.7 is very striking, we think you'll agree, more so than it would have been had it been represented as a bar chart.

As well as all the reservations about sample size and representativeness that we've previously discussed, what you have to beware of with a pictogram is that, since it uses the symbol of a three-dimensional object, difference in size is represented in three dimensions rather than one as it would be on bar chart. In Figure 2.1.7 this exaggerates the difference between the male and female averages. For example, the difference in heart volume between untrained men and women is 24.1 per cent but the untrained woman looks probably half the size of the man since she is not only 24 per cent shorter but proportioned to that height. If you imagine these symbols as bar graphs, all of the same thickness, you will get a different impression of the relative differences. Birke has chosen this pictogram because it gives a strong impression of the effects of training, but this is because it exaggerates them, and unfortunately it also exaggerates the sex difference. Pictograms usually do this: be careful how you read them, especially when they illustrate differences between men and women. But do not necessarily avoid them, they can make a point very dramatically as they do in the maps in Book Three, but they must be read with care.

> Now finish studying Article 2.1 (pp. 95–102), making notes on the following.
>
> What are some of the physical differences between male and female brains and why is it a problem to draw conclusions about gender difference from them?
>
> What are the problems of researching physiological differences between brains?

Birke finishes with a section on sex differences in human brains, examining both their physiology and their function. This is an important area because justifications for unequal performance between men and women in activities such as school science or professional engineering are no longer always grounded in assertions about women's physical incapacity to work in a lab or handle machinery, but in assertions that women's innate mental functioning (for example, poor spatial awareness, as measured in tests) means that they have less ability to do certain intellectual activities. These kind of causal associations are very questionable.

Birke looks at just how difficult it is to relate brain function to specific behaviour, and to observe brain function in a healthy, undamaged brain. She demonstrates that there is often an explicit acceptance of gender difference in the minds of researchers before the search for evidence of physiological sex difference begins. Often more open-minded interpretation of empirical evidence about biologically based sex differences (other than reproductive function) demonstrates that the sexes are more similar than they are different.

Thinking about empirical evidence

We have asked you to spend a long time on Birke's article. This is because her arguments and her empirical evidence are important, as well as the statistical methods she uses to illustrate the evidence. Throughout this Study Guide we are hoping to encourage in you a critical perspective on empirical evidence. Empirical data are, in theory, the foundation of modern science, although you will by now be familiar with the fact that feminist writing often questions whether this has really been the case. To use empirical data well yourself and to be able to evaluate other people's use of such data, it is important to begin by asking some very simple questions.

1   How has the phenomenon under investigation been defined: some things are simple (such as weight, height), others are open to debate (such as strength, intelligence, creativity)?

2   How has the phenomenon been measured: some things are directly observable and have tools designed for them (weighing scales, tape measures), others are measured indirectly through observing other associated factors (brain function)?

3   How have the measurements (the raw data) been collected: how many events have been measured, when, by whom?

4   How have the raw data been processed? (This is often through some kind of statistical technique which allows large amounts of raw data to be handled.)

5   How have the data been represented (maps, graphs, tables etc.)?

It is possible at any of these points in the process that either the research procedure is wrong – for example the measuring instrument is not the right one or the statistical test chosen is inappropriate – or that the procedure is correct but inaccurate. Even if you are satisfied, as far as you can be, that the empirical evidence is well-founded, it may not follow that the arguments for which it is being used have any real connection with it.

Summary: feminism and the biological bases of gender

Biological determinism, used to justify gender difference and the legal and social inequality of women, was one of the first areas of science to be criticized by feminism. The first feminist attacks took the form of arguing that the social determinants of gender difference were so strong that biology could effectively be ignored. But for many women this denied the experience of the internal processes of their own bodies; it also ignored medical developments such as the use of chemical hormones to alter the body's physiology and its function. It became necessary for feminism not only to have a sophisticated model of the interaction of biology and the environment, but for feminists to grapple with the evidence about biological sex difference.

In the next reading you will examine feminist critiques of another scientific discipline, that of anthropology, which has been another source of biologistic justifications for gender difference.

2.3 ORIGINS, ANTHROPOLOGY AND FEMINISM

We can look for the origins of gender differences in the biology of human beings; we can also look for them in the evolution of human societies – through anthropology. Anthropology is in its widest sense the science of human beings, and has several branches within it. The main division is between physical anthropology and social or cultural anthropology. Physical anthropology focuses on human beings as animals in order to understand human behaviour in terms of the behaviour of other mammals. Another major branch is concerned to understand early hominid behaviour and looks at the fossil record. Physical anthropology draws heavily on evolutionary theory. Social or cultural anthropology is concerned with understanding contemporary human societies and ethnographers study existing human groups.

Homo sapiens is classified as a species of ape, more evolutionarily advanced, many would argue, than other apes, but an ape nevertheless, and therefore the study of common patterns in the biology and behaviour of apes will provide insight into human behaviour. The following paragraphs are taken from Desmond Morris's introduction to his popular book of the late 1960s, *The Naked Ape*. Its implicit ideology of the 'natural' and its prioritizing of males as the subjects of study have made Morris an obvious target for feminist criticism.

> There are one hundred and ninety-three living species of monkeys and apes. One hundred and ninety-two of them are covered with hair. The exception is a naked ape self-named *Homo sapiens*. This unusual and highly successful species spends a great deal of time examining his higher motives and an equal amount of time studiously ignoring his fundamental ones. He is proud that he has the biggest brain of all the primates, but attempts to conceal the fact that he also has the biggest penis, preferring to accord this honour falsely to the mighty gorilla. He is an intensely vocal, acutely exploratory, over-crowded ape, and it is high time we examined his basic behaviour.

> I am a zoologist and the naked ape is an animal. He is therefore fair game for my pen ... [I]n becoming so erudite, *Homo sapiens* has remained a naked ape nevertheless; in acquiring lofty new motives, he has lost none of the earthy old ones. This is frequently a cause of some embarrassment to him, but his old impulses have been with him for millions of years, his new ones only for a few thousand at the most – and there is no hope of quickly shrugging off the accumulated genetic legacy of his whole evolutionary past. He would be a far less worried and more fulfilled animal if only he would face up to this fact.
>
> (Morris, 1967, p. 9)

Morris's notion that we should throw off the repression of culture and respond to our natural (i.e. ape-like) instincts sounds, from the vantage point of the 1990s, to reflect very much the spirit of the 1960s. And his choice of penis size as a criterion of what makes *Homo sapiens* different from other apes reflects the fact that he was writing before the advent of the second wave of feminism.

Ten years later another zoologist, an American, David Barash, wrote a similar popular text on the subject, which by then had a new label which appeared in the title of his book, *Sociobiology: the whisperings within* (1980). He was more circumspect in his writing, since a feminist critique of sociobiology had developed in the years between which he had to acknowledge.

The other main branch of physical anthropology studies the remains of artefacts and fossils in order to build a picture of the evolutionary stages of the development of human beings as a species and of hominid societies. These early hominids are pictured as evolutionary bridges between ape-like creatures and human beings. Information from the study of present-day primates is used to speculate about the behaviour of these prehistoric ancestors of human beings. It was in this search for the origins of human social behaviour that 'Man the Hunter' emerged.

Article 2.2 'The changing role of women in models of human evolution' by Linda Marie Fedigan

In Book Three Linda Marie Fedigan synthesizes a critique of these three aspects of anthropology for their gendered bias, and she goes on to speculate about how the subject might have produced different models of human evolution if it had been written by women and people from non-Western societies.

Modelling gender roles in early human societies

> Turn to Article 2.2 and read the Introduction and the section entitled 'Historical context' (pp. 103–12). Make notes on the following.
>
> What contradictions exist in Darwin's theory of sexual selection?
>
> What do you understand by the 'coat-tails' theory of evolution?
>
> What are the similarities between Darwin's model of sexual selection and the model of 'Man the Hunter'?
>
> Summarize the 'Woman the Gatherer' model of Zihlman.
>
> How does the 'sharing' model attempt to integrate both the previous models?
>
> How does Lovejoy's model differ from all the others and why does Fedigan see him as attempting to invalidate more 'feminist' models?
>
> The final model Fedigan presents is that of Leibowitz, which is significantly different from all the others – in what way?

Darwin's nineteenth-century theory of the workings of sexual selection remain central to twentieth-century ethologists such as Morris and Barash. It is interesting to look at some of Darwin's original writing from *On the Origin of Species by means of Natural Selection*, published in 1859, to see the power he credited to sexual selection, and the combative model he held of sexuality. The animal world is perceived as a battlefield.

ACTIVITY 10

Read the following passage and pick out those words and phrases which demonstrate this war metaphor.

This form of selection depends, not on a struggle for existence in relation to other organic beings or to external conditions, but on a struggle between the individuals of one sex, generally the males, for the possession of the other sex. The result is not death to the unsuccessful competitor, but few or no offspring. Sexual selection is, therefore, less rigorous than natural selection. Generally, the most vigorous males, those which are best fitted for their places in nature, will leave most progeny. But in many cases, victory depends not so much on general vigour, as on having special weapons, confined to the male sex ... Sexual selection, by always allowing the victor to breed, might surely give indomitable courage, length to the spur, and strength to the wing ...

... The war is, perhaps, severest between the males of polygamous animals, and these seem oftenest provided with special weapons. The males of carnivorous animals are already well armed; though to them and to others, special means of defence may be given through means of sexual selection, as the mane to the lion, and the hooked jaw to the male salmon; for the shield may be as important for victory as the sword or spear ...

COMMENT

I hope you noted words like 'victory', the 'victor', 'weapons', 'courage', 'war', being 'armed', 'shield', and that these words were used only of male animals. When females select, Darwin argued, they do so according to standards of 'beauty'. In both cases the males are seen in competition with each other, to 'possess' the females. It is obvious why a model of evolution which can be used to reinforce the naturalness of stereotypical gender behaviour should be attacked by feminists.

The twentieth-century models described by Fedigan explore the effect of social evolution in producing a gendered society. It is argued that group survival and individual survival are absolutely dependent on each other, and that a sexual division of labour provides the optimum conditions for food supply. You do not need to identify the researchers named by Fedigan but you need to understand the difference between the models of 'Man the Hunter', 'Woman the Gatherer'

Figure 6
'Man the Hunter'

and 'sharing', and the different ways in which the models interpret similar evidence. Leibowitz's argument is most interesting from the perspective of many of the articles in the later chapters of *Inventing Women*. She sees the sexual division of labour as resulting from the development of particular kinds of technology, and that this occurred relatively late in evolutionary terms, before which males and females engaged in the same kinds of food-producing activities.

The anthropological evidence

Read the section entitled 'The primate evidence' (pp. 112–14), noting how evidence from the study of baboons is used to support a 'Man the Hunter' model and that from chimpanzees to support a 'Woman the Gatherer' model.

Read the section on 'The ethnographic evidence' (pp. 114–16), making notes on arguments against using ethnographic evidence from contemporary peoples to reconstruct early human life, and arguments for doing so.

Does the ethnographic evidence support the model of the productive or of the dependent female?

Read the section on 'The material evidence' (pp. 117–18). In what way is Pott's interpretation of the anthropological evidence from the Olduvai Gorge and Koobi-Fora supportive of feminist models of the roles of females in early human societies?

The three sections you have just read demonstrate the ways in which evidence can be used to support opposing theoretical models. They show how it is important to gather more evidence through detailed field research. It also has to be recognized that new evidence never conclusively settles any debate. The nature of ethnographic data and models based on them is the most contested.

To nineteenth-century anthropologists, white men and industrialized Western society were more evolved than other societies and there was a sense of racial superiority in some writings. This implicit racism is now questioned by ethnographers, especially feminists. The ethnographer Lila Abu-Lughod identifies anthropology as being heavily involved with racism and sexism:

> Anthropology and feminism as academic practices are two disciplines which arise out of and focus on the two fundamental and political systems of difference on which the unequal world of modern capitalism has historically depended: race and gender. Both are rooted in and deal with the problem of historically constituted self/other distinctions. But they come at the issue of self and other from different places within the structure of difference. Anthropological discourse, with its roots in the exploration and colonization of the rest of the world by the West, is the discourse of the self. It defines itself primarily as the study of the other, which means that its selfhood was not problematic. Some would even argue that the Western civilized self was constituted in part through this confrontation with and picturing of the savage or primitive other.

(Abu-Lughod, 1991, p. 24)

Why bother to search for origins?

Now read the 'Conclusion' of Fedigan's article (pp. 119–22). Why does Fedigan feel that it is worth looking for 'origins' and do you agree with her? Think of all the origins theories/myths/stories that you are familiar with: do you feel that they have reinforced gender inequality, or have ever been personally oppressive to you?

Summarize in your own words what Fedigan describes Landau as saying about the imaginative narrative element of anthropology. This relates to theories about the construction of knowledge through language that you will meet later in the course. (You might find this a useful example when you come to study Foucault and discourse.)

Fedigan argues that origins stories have important symbolic value to a society and that, as far as is known, all human societies have origins myths. At an individual level the popular interest in family trees and 'roots' displays the psychological satisfaction of a personal search for origins. Modern industrialized societies have attempted to turn the symbolic narrative into a scientific activity, through anthropology, but also through other sciences such as physics and astronomy where the search is for the origins of the universe. However, you may argue that societies would be better off without origins stories of any sort, and that they should perhaps focus their intellectual and technical energies into making the future instead.

Many women have found Western origins myths to be very oppressive in the role given to women. We, the Study Guide authors, were soaked in the Judeo-Christian myth of Adam and Eve and the Garden of Eden in our childhoods, and in our schools we were introduced to the mythic Greek tales of violent male gods who created the world by dismembering each other and raping and/or dismembering female gods. None of these has very creative roles for women.

▶ **ACTIVITY 11** ◀

You may have cultural roots which give you access to other traditions; if so, think about the role of women in them, and share your insights with others in your tutorial group to see whether there are any origins myths which give the central, positive role to women.

The nature of the narrative – in anthropology, a particular narrative (that of the hero's tale) – is an illustration of the way a discourse moulds our perception of the world. Fedigan notes that no matter how the empirical evidence was analysed, 'Man the Hero' seemed immovable as a central figure in any model. She seems to be suggesting that the strength of this myth is in great part due to the fact that men have dominated anthropology. Like Abu-Lughod, she argues that feminist women see the world differently and would create different narratives.

2.4 MEDICINE: A MASCULINE SCIENCE

Controversies about health and health care have been a familiar feature of the last thirty years. Some of these have concerned medical treatment or interventions specific to women, such as the side-effects of contraception and of hormone replacement therapy or the technology of childbirth. At the time of writing this Study Guide, there was a controversy about the value of breast self-examination, begun by the British Government's former Chief Medical Officer who declared in 1991 that self-examination did not lead to the detection of cancerous tissue. After some days during which leaflets describing self-examination were withdrawn, and many women lost confidence in the simple examination techniques they were using on themselves, the Government reversed its advice. See Figure 7.

The profession of medicine has been traditionally a male preserve and, although the NHS is one of the largest employers of women in the UK, in the 1980s women were 90 per cent of all nursing staff, but only 22 per cent of all doctors, 13 per cent of hospital consultants and 1 per cent of general surgeons.

As well as being a male-dominated profession medicine has produced definitions of illness and health and descriptions of disease which have contained a particular model of biology in which a healthy woman's body is seen as deficient. In the 1980s this deficiency might be seen as hormonal; in

Ministers make U-turn on breast cancer testing

**by Michael Durham
Social Affairs Correspondent**

WOMEN are to be told by the Department of Health to continue examining themselves for breast cancer, despite recent official advice to the contrary. New guidelines on the disease, which kills 13,000 women a year, will overturn the advice of the government's former chief medical officer, Sir Donald Acheson, who said self-examination was a waste of time.

His successor, Professor Kenneth Calman, will intervene to end concern caused by Acheson, who claimed there was "substantial evidence" that the checks were ineffective and could give a false sense of security.

Experts believe that up to eight in 10 of the 25,000 new cases of breast cancer each year are detected as a result of self-examination.

The advice, to be published on Tuesday, was welcomed this weekend by doctors and patients' groups, who said that women had been left confused about how to protect themselves against the second-biggest cause of female death in Britain.

Yesterday Virginia Bottomley, the health minister, said the revised guidelines had been compiled as quickly as possible because of the uncertainty. "The new chief medical officer has urgently reviewed the guidelines and I am now acting swiftly to clarify the situation," she said.

Bottomley refused to accept that Acheson had blundered, but said she wanted to reassure women that they could help to protect themselves against cancer. "I shall simply be encouraging women to be aware of any changes in their bodies, and to report any uncertainties they may have to their doctors," she said.

Acheson, who retired two weeks ago, was on holiday and unavailable for comment.

In his first public statement since becoming chief medical officer, Calman will emphasise the importance of self-examination, especially for women under 50 who are not entitled to regular breast X-rays. Last year more than 6,000 women under 50 contracted the disease.

Leaflets to be circulated by the end of the year will tell women to:
● check the general shape and outline of the breasts for any obvious malformations;
● make a physical examination for lumps;
● observe the nipples, particularly for any changes such as a "pulled-in" look, inversion, bleeding or discharge.

Unlike previous self-examination instructions, the new, simpler guidelines do not recommend regular monthly checks. Women will be told to conduct them whenever they choose, perhaps every few months.

Yesterday breast cancer specialists welcomed what they said amounted to backtracking by the government. "This seems to be a U-turn, without saying it in so many words," said Robert Mansel, professor of surgery at Withington hospital, Manchester. "This will help to put the matter straight."

The Women's National Cancer Control Campaign also supported the new advice: "It will clear up the confusion which has made a lot of women very anxious over the last few days."

'We now have substantial evidence that Sir Donald Acheson is a waste of time.'

Figure 7
Source: *The Sunday Times*, 29 September 1991

medieval or even Victorian Britain the deficiency was of 'vital energy'. For example, Thomas Aquinas (1225-1274) wrote:

> As regards the individual nature, women is defective and misbegotten, for the active force in the male seed tends to the production of a perfect likeness in the masculine sex; while the production of woman comes from a defect in the active force or from some maternal indisposition, or even from some external influence ...

(from *Summa Theologica*, quoted in O'Faolain and Martines, 1979)

Defining and identifying health

▶ **ACTIVITY 12** ◀

Stop for a moment and think about your own body and your sense of health or well-being. If you are a woman, have you ever had a sense of a particular state of 'female' physical well-being, and, on the other hand, a state of female 'non-well-being'?

COMMENT

The second part of that question was probably the easier to answer. Many of us are likely to have had/or still have times in our menstrual cycles when we certainly don't have a sense of physical well-being, and which we relate directly to the processes of our *female* bodies. But does this constitute illness, and what point does it become something that you look for a medical remedy for? Describing a particular state of female well-being was harder for us and probably for you. The one we came up with was the middle period of pregnancy – after the sickness ended and before we got heartburn and our ankles became swollen. But what does this say about our sensations of our bodily selves: that we associate sensations of specific female bodily processes, for example menstruation, with feeling ill? Is this due to the social construction of our bodily processes and, if so, can we change the way we not only think about them, but feel them?

Defining what constitutes illness is not only a problem of making sense of our subjective bodily feelings, it is also a problem with respect to indicating the well-being of societies and populations.

Penny Kane in her book, *Women's Health: from womb to tomb* (1991), spends a chapter looking at demographic indicators of illness such as surveys of self-reported illness, doctors' visits, medicines prescribed, hospital referrals, drug prescription rates and others. Most of these she finds are influenced by gender in such a way that it is difficult to obtain comparisons between men and women. She writes:

> … the use of the oral contraceptive pill accounted for four-fifths of differential medication between women and men. Hospital beds, and the time of general practitioners, are also occupied for normal healthy pregnancies, and for contraception and sterilization …
>
> … The use of contraception has nothing to do with being ill. Having a baby is a natural female function and, unless there are complications, it too has nothing to do with being ill. Yet the presented statistics seldom separate out these events, presumably because those who analyse them or use them seldom notice that they are based on a false assumption. The assumption – that taking a pill, or visiting a doctor, implies some health problem – probably does hold true for men. It is patently untrue for women.

(Kane, 1991, pp. 85, 86)

▶ **ACTIVITY 13** ◀

Now think about times when you have visited a doctor. How do you usually feel? Do you say what you want to say, ask the questions you want to ask, get all the information that you want? If not, why not?

COMMENT

It is common for both women and men to be in awe of or intimidated by a medical doctor. The power and authority vested in medical practitioners is enormous, both in modern scientific medicine and in pre-scientific and alternative medicine. This may be partly because the experience of illness is also one of powerlessness over one's own body, and this is then multiplied by the mystique of expertise granted to the doctor. This situation can be made worse for women when that expertise includes a model of female biology as diseased or deficient as well as an ideology of the social role of women as dependent, weak and needy.

> We have not yet asked you to read the Introduction to Chapter 2 in Book Three (pp. 73–80). This is a very good time to do so. As you read, make notes on the following.
>
> What is being argued about the relation between 'Nature' and 'Woman'?
>
> What is gender dysphoria? (This issue is explored further in Radio 06.)
>
> Use the review of Birke and Fedigan in the Introduction as a way of revising what you have just read.
>
> In your own words describe a feminist critique of medicine.
>
> The issue of 'contradictory reality' is an important one, and is a major part of the argument in the article by Riessman that you will be studying next.
>
> Read the discussion on the production and marketing of drugs and devices. How does this expand your model of medicine?
>
> We will discuss Maps 1, 2 and 3 later in the Study Guide. At this point you could profitably spend some time establishing the scale of comparisons between rich and poor countries.

Article 2.3 'Women and medicalization: a new perspective' by Catherine Kohler Riessman

> What is the medicalization of health?
>
> *Key concepts*
>
> medicalization   pathology/pathological
> deviance
>
> Read the first two sections of Article 2.3, the introduction and the section entitled 'The medicalization framework' (pp. 123–6). Make notes on the following.
>
> In the first section Riessman summarizes the feminist critique of medicine but suggests that it has not properly conceptualized the role of women. What is her criticism, and what motives does she attribute to doctors and to women?
>
> In your own words make notes on what the term 'medicalization' means, and the levels on which it occurs.
>
> Riessman argues that there are three ways in which scientific method constrains medical knowledge and practice, what are they?
>
> Why is deviance an important concept in medicine?
>
> Riessman argues that relatively powerless groups in society (she calls them 'structurally dependent populations') are more likely to be classified as sick. Note some examples of your own, if you can.
>
> How does class complicate a gender analysis of medicine?

Reissman argues that feminist critics of medicine have conceived of women as 'victims', deprived of both knowledge and power as patients and practitioners, but women have at times been active in constructing new definitions and promoting new techniques. Doctors (and others involved in medicine such as producers of medical technology or drugs) are motivated to increase the power of the profession of which they are members, and to keep themselves in profit. Women are also driven by their economic needs and their subordinate social role, but their class allegiance may cause them to support the interests of professionals.

By medicalization Reissman is referring to both the definition of people as being 'healthy' or 'sick', and the way in which this knowledge is then used to deal with 'sickness' and people who are 'sick'. She sees it happen at the *conceptual* level – the construction of medical knowledge, the *institutional* level – how hospitals organize treatment, and at the *interpersonal* level – how doctors treat patients. She sees scientific method as constraining medical knowledge because bias enters in the choice of problem to study. Complex processes are reduced to deterministic cause-and-effect models and things outside the model are ignored. Finally, the use of scientific method – even if inappropriate – is a badge of authority for the doctor. By now you should be familiar with this kind of criticism of scientific method in general.

Whether relatively powerless groups are categorized wrongly as sick or whether they are actually made sick by their powerless position – usually accompanied by economic deprivation – is an important debate, and this is also why it is important to have good indicators of the quality of health of a population, and of groups within a population – such as women.

The medicalization of childbirth and abortion

Key concepts

cultural authority   medical management of childbirth
social childbirth   demedicalization

Read the sections of Article 2.3 entitled 'Childbirth' and 'Abortion' (pp. 126–32). Make notes on:

- the reasons why middle-class women promoted 'scientific childbirth'. Reissman does not credit working-class women with also promoting the doctors' role, but can you think of good reasons why they might?
- the reasons why medical practitioners promoted 'scientific childbirth'
- the frequency of occurrence of abortion in the USA in the nineteenth century and who was involved in it
- the reasons why women campaigned to outlaw abortion.

Reissman is describing the particular historical context of the United States. The process of the professionalization of medicine was completed much earlier in the United Kingdom and by the nineteenth century women were restricted to midwifery and nursing, and unqualified men could not practise as doctors.

Reissman is critical – in common with many feminist writers, and with the pressure groups for 'natural' childbirth – of the expansion of medical intervention into all childbirth, and the way this defines childbirth as 'pathological'. But she also goes on to look at why women, initially at least, promoted this.

It was middle-class women, she argued, who promoted interventions in labour and the use of pain relief, partly because they were asserting their right not to have to suffer. Queen Victoria lent support to the campaign by praising the use of chloroform during her own labour with some of her children. Working-class women, such as those who wrote to Margaret Llewelyn Davies in 1914 (Davies, 1915/1978), understood that it was their general state of ill-health and overwork which contributed to the complications they experienced in their pregnancies, and the huge infant mortality they reported. Of the women who wrote to her in 1914, 348 gave definite figures; of these 148 or 42.2 per cent had had still births or miscarriages (some had had both). Of the 52 who had stillbirths, nine women had 2 stillbirths each and one woman 5 stillbirths. 86 women (24.7 per cent) lost children in the first year of life. This contradicts Reissman's statement that 'childbirth is an event that occurs without complications in most cases', at least as far as historical data are concerned. Davies' sample believed that they and their children would have a safer labour if assisted by a doctor. They saved carefully from very small incomes to be able to pay for one to attend the birth, and only chose a midwife if they could not afford the doctor's fee. Their letters were used in the Campaign by the Women's Co-operative Guild to improve maternal and infant care through local government provision of health centres and health visitors as well as state provision of maternity benefit.

Reduction in maternal mortality has been the biggest improvement in women's health in the industrialized world over the last fifty years (Kane, 1991). In Australia, for example, in the 1920s deaths due to childbirth were among the five main causes of death among women in the 25–44 year age group. In the 1980s less than one woman in 10,000 died in childbirth. Kane includes improved ante-natal and post-natal care amongst a list of contributing factors, as well as the reduction in the numbers of children born. Hospitals have become 'centres of excellence' for childbirth despite the fact that the need for medical intervention in childbirth is considerably less than it was in 1914. Reissman discusses how an increased demand by women for more 'natural' childbirth and less high technology intervention has led to 'natural' childbirth becoming an area of medical expertise which happens in specially designed labour rooms in hospitals.

Maternal mortality in underdeveloped countries

The following table and commentary are taken from a 1986 Survey of Bangladesh (quoted in Kane, 1991). Look at them and then answer the questions below.

The survey, in two areas of rural Bangladesh, recorded 9317 live births and 58 maternal deaths, giving a maternal mortality rate of 62.3 per 10,000 live births, in contrast to less than one per 10,000 in England and Wales in 1984. Maternal deaths accounted for almost half (46 per cent) of all deaths of women aged 15-44, and within this age-range were most common in older women. The maternal mortality rate per 10,000 live births increased to 178 among those aged 35-39, and 250 among those over 40. Only a handful of those who died had been taken to any kind of health centre or hospital when they became ill.

Table 3 Most common causes of maternal death in two rural areas of Bangladesh, 1982–83

Cause	Per cent of deaths
Eclampsia	20.7
Septic abortion	20.7
Post-partum sepsis	10.3
Obstructed labour	10.3
Haemorrhage	10.3
Others	27.7

Source: Kane, 1991, pp. 40–1

► **ACTIVITY 14** ◄

Looking at the extract and Table 3, what is:

(a) the comparison of maternal deaths in a rich industrial nation and those in a poor non-industrial nation?

(b) the proportion of maternal deaths due to unsafe abortion?

What conclusions, if any, can you draw from the figures?

COMMENT

You should have picked out that the ratio of maternal mortality in Bangladesh to that in the UK is 62:1.

Although a figure of 20.7 per cent is given for death due to septic abortion, when abortion is illegal it can be difficult to obtain accurate figures and death is more likely to be categorized as due to another cause; it could therefore be even larger than stated.

► **ACTIVITY 15** ◄

Turn to Maps 1a and 1b in the colour plate section of Book Three. Although the maps are small you should be able to identify those countries with high maternal and infant mortality. Compare this map to Map 2 which shows the frequency of contraceptive use.

COMMENT

You will see that some countries have high levels of contraceptive use as well as high levels of maternal and infant mortality – in particular, South American countries. Therefore the relationship is not direct but involves other factors such as poverty and the availability of health care, perhaps as well as ideology about maternity and sexuality.

The medicalization of menstruation, weight and depression

Key concepts

premenstrual syndrome*(PMS) also   psychotropic drugs
called premenstrual tension (PMT)

social etiology**   psychotherapy

(Note:
*a syndrome is simply a combination of symptoms associated with a particular disease
**etiology is the study of causes of a disease.)

> Now go back to Article 2.3 and read 'Medicalization of women's lives', 'Premenstrual syndrome', 'The medical beauty business' and 'Medicalization and psychiatry' (pp. 132–40), making notes on the following.
>
> What does Riessman think are the reasons for the medical profession creating PMS?
>
> What other groups have been involved in supporting the existence of PMS and why?
>
> What have the contradictions been for women with respect to PMS?
>
> Why does Riessman see the medicalization of 'obesity' as being so oppressive for women?
>
> What does she mean by 'individualizing the problem of weight'?

> What does Reissman mean by describing psychotherapy as 'depoliticizing' issues? If you have ever experienced psychotherapy you might want to reflect on your experience and consider whether you agree with Riessman.

Riessman's discussion of the creation of a biological standard against which women are measured, should have made you think about Birke's discussion of distributions of characteristics in populations; that absolute measures of maleness and femaleness do not exist, and neither do absolute measures of health. Because of this it is possible to identify large groups of people whose bodily processes or sensations on any indicator do not match a constructed 'healthy' response. The question remains whether this is an indication of illness. In these sections Riessman identifies three particular aspects of women's lives – menstrual cycle, weight and what may crudely be described as 'misery' – that have become defined as medical problems with medical treatment. In all three she sees the medical profession imposing a model of a 'healthy' woman, i.e. one with few or no uncomfortable indications of their menstrual cycle, and who is thin and contented, and she argues that women have colluded in creating this stereotype by asking for medical treatment if they don't correspond to it. She sees other groups – most importantly food and drugs manufacturers – as supporting this model in order to market their products. Riessman also sees the involvement of other agencies such as the legal profession (PMS) and the fashion and sports industry (obesity). But trends in treatment change: in 1951 a woman might have been recommended Horlicks for her exhaustion and depression (see Figure 8); by the 1970s she might have been prescribed psychotropic drugs; and by the 1990s psychotherapy might be suggested.

It is easier to see that for some women the effects of depression or hormonal irregularities are dramatic, and they have benefited from their conditions being acknowledged. Riessman worries that when they are acknowledged as medical problems they are individualized, that is seen as a problem residing with the individual rather than as social problem; the individual is then treated rather than an attempt being made to bring about social change. This is what she means by 'depoliticizing' an issue. As feminists during the 1980s have become more sympathetic towards psychoanalytical tools, many would be less critical of therapy or analysis as depoliticizing, and instead see it as a tool to gain access to those aspects of our unconscious which fetter our ability to act.

Medicine as a conflict of interests

> Now read the last two sections of Article 2.3 (pp. 140–44). This is where Riessman generalizes from her specific examples the advantages and disadvantages that have accrued to women from the medicalization of their lives.
>
> List the advantages accruing to the medical professionals from this.
>
> List the advantages and disadvantages accruing to women.
>
> Have men's lives been medicalized; if so, to what extent?
>
> Near the end of the article Riessman gives a definition of what demedicalization would mean. Is it clear to you how this differs from 'deprofessionalization' discussed in the footnote?

Riessman identifies medicine as a product of a capitalist economy and a technologically dominated medical care system. However, the opening up of socialist countries in the early 1990s revealed socialist medical care systems which suffered from all the problems identified by Riessman, aggravated by economic collapse. The criticism of the system being technology driven, however, seems to hold across countries and cultures.

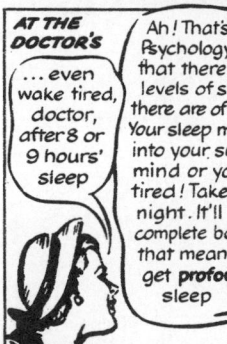

Figure 8
Advertisement for Horlicks (*Picture Post*, 27 October 1951)

She does think that men's lives have been medicalized: she lists hyperactivity in male children, addiction, and occupation-related conditions. However, she argues that men's lives have not been transformed in the same way as women's; male characteristics/behaviour are less likely to be seen as pathological. The contradiction for women is that we have seen freedom of choice over the biological processes of our lives as liberating but in searching for them through medical solutions we have had that freedom of choice curtailed. At the conclusion of the article Riessman argues that to demedicalize is 'not to deny the biological components of experience but to alter the ownership, production and use of scientific knowledge.' Although she tries to make a distinction between this and deprofessionalization in her footnote, it is hard to see a clear distinction. At the end of the article she is careful to argue that what is wanted is a revolution in the models on which medicine is based, while at the same time recognizing that good health care is of importance to women.

2.5 REPRODUCTION: CONTROL, CONTRACEPTION AND ABORTION

Feminist movements have all contained some element of campaigning for women to have control over their reproduction. In the first wave this took two forms: one was to campaign for control over male sexuality by the use of abstinence. Christobel Pankhurst and early suffrage leaders promoted this. From the viewpoint of the 1990s this may appear to be a very radical feminist demand, but, as we indicated in the discussion of Margaret Llewelyn Davies' work, it was more acceptable to a social ideology which saw sex as being without pleasure for women and part of the 'baser' nature of men. The other campaign (promoted by women such as Marie Stopes in the UK and Margaret Sanger in the USA) was for women to be given access to the technology of birth control, which in the early part of this century meant appliances such as condoms and diaphragms. By the second wave of feminism in the 1970s contraception was freely available in the UK and its use was promoted in many industrialized countries. Contraceptive technology has probably been the technology which has had the most direct impact on women's lives in the twentieth century. It gives women the potential to choose if and when to have children, and to disconnect sexual activity from procreation if we choose. It also has controversial side-effects both personal and social, and it is not completely reliable. The following activity explores failure rates for different methods of contraception.

► **ACTIVITY 16** ◄

The following table is taken from *Our Bodies, Our Selves* (1976), the archetypal self-help health handbook for women. It gives this table in a chapter aimed at helping women in the mid 1970s to make choices about which birth control method to use. Note that theoretical failure rate is based on a hypothetical perfect use of the method (usually quoted by the manufacturer) and actual use is based on records over time. This includes accidents, forgetting or improper use. It is equivalent to comparing failure in a controlled experimental situation with failure in the real world.

Which methods had high failure rates and for which was there a large discrepancy between theoretical and actual failure?

Table 4 Approximate failure rate (pregnancies per 100 woman years)†

	Theoretical failure rate	Actual use failure rate
Abortion	0+	0+*
Abstinence	0	?
Hysterectomy	0.0001	0.0001
Tubal ligation	0.04	0.04
Vasectomy	Less than 0.15	0.15
Oral contraceptives (combined)	Less than 1.0	2-5
I.M. long-acting progestin	Less than 1.0	5-10
Condom + spermicidal agent	1.0	5
Low-dose oral progestin	1-4	5-10
IUD	1-5	6
Condom	3	15-20
Diaphragm	3	20-25
Spermicidal foam	3	30
Coitus interruptus	15	20-25
Rhythm (calendar)	15	35
Lactation for 12 months	15	40
Chance (sexually active)	80	80

Notes:
† Emory University Family Planning Program, *Contraceptive Technology 1974-1975*
* Among women actually depending upon abortion as a means of fertility control, effectiveness is less than 100 per cent as in some instances women change their minds.
Source: The Boston Women's Health Book Collective, 1976, p. 185

'Free abortion on demand. A woman's right to choose' was one of the main demands of second wave feminism. Contraception was not foolproof; to be in control of your contraception (it was argued), safe legal abortion was necessary as a back-up. In 1967 the Abortion Act legalized abortion in England, Wales and Scotland, but made the decision to allow abortion a medical one. Two doctors had to agree that the risks of continuing a pregnancy were greater than if it was terminated: the risks to be considered were to a woman's life, her health – mental or physical, risk of serious abnormality in the foetus and risk to existing children. All aspects of abortion are medicalized and what became known as the 'right to choose' campaign was an attack on this.

▶ **ACTIVITY 17** ◀

We are aware that for many people discussion of abortion is very distressing, either because of strongly held moral or religious convictions, or because you are one of the many women who have been faced with the issue of whether to seek an abortion – for whatever reason (or you are the partner of a woman who has). Our aim is not to change minds, nor can we do much to help you deal with the memory of a traumatic experience; however, since we believe that these personal issues could get in the way of your thinking about the data and arguments we present,

> we suggest that rather than ignoring them you spend a little time with your Personal Workbook examining them explicitly, and writing them down as a way of getting clear about them. If you find your personal memories very distressing, you might like to think about getting counselling, since it is now recognized that some women who willingly choose abortion can later feel very distressed about it. The British Pregnancy Advisory Council will recommend a counsellor.

Abortion should not be thought of as only a back-up to contraception. Look again at Map 2 in the colour plate section in Book Three. In South American countries the percentage of women using contraception is small – under 15 per cent – yet in Bolivia and Ecuador the number of abortions is very high: in Bolivia the estimate is that one quarter of women have had an abortion, and figures for illegal abortions in these countries are quoted as higher than countries with liberal abortion laws (Seager and Olson, 1986).

The concept of reproductive rights

Resistance to the legalization of abortion in the past was based on religious and ethical beliefs about the sanctity of life, as well as moral beliefs about sexuality. In the original UK legislation there was theoretically no specified time-limit for an abortion in terms of foetal development, but the viability of the foetus was the actual limit. In 1990 the legislation was changed to reduce the time limit to 24 weeks except for special cases. This change was not due to anti-abortionists winning the moral or ethical arguments but to developments in the care of premature babies such that babies beyond 24 weeks gestation now have a significant chance of survival. In effect developments in technology have led to a changed perception of what constitutes a viable foetus both actually and legally. At the same time developments in technology have provided techniques to aid conception amongst women and men who are in practice infertile. In vitro fertilization – test-tube babies – was one of the media events of the 1980s. Feminists now identified *conception* as an area in which medicalization needed to be resisted. The original 'right to choose' slogan presumed that women were fertile and that children were a problem. There was little discussion about what constituted choice for infertile women, and little apparent sympathy. Some of this attitude can be explained by the age of women active in the Women's Liberation Movement of the early 1970s, most of whom were too young to be aware of their own infertility or that of their friends. It was an awareness that in places women from poor countries and those from ethnic minorities were being pressurized into accepting sterilization or injectable contraceptives that first raised the issue of 'reproductive rights'. The apparently sudden developments in reproductive technology reinforced the need for a concept which covered all aspects of reproduction in a coordinated way. This is summarized by Marge Berer:

> The phrase 'women's reproductive rights' to describe the concept of women's right to decide if, when and how to have children has only been around since about 1979. It was first coined in the USA by feminists who formed the campaigning Reproductive Rights National Network. The concept itself is new in that it links up all the different aspects of birth control and childbearing which previously had been campaigned on separately by women. Stretching back into the nineteenth century in Britain we can find many campaigns organized by women: for the use of condoms to prevent sexually transmitted diseases, for safer childbirth, for the right to information about how to practise birth control and for free access to birth-control methods, and more recently, campaigns for legal abortion. The common thread in these campaigns is that they have been single issues, with specific objectives in relation to one main aspect of women's lack of autonomous control over reproduction. As such they have had a great measure of success in achieving their aims ...

However, in spite of these vast gains, women have not achieved, either in law or in widespread social and medical thought or practice, the acceptance of a right to control over our own reproduction. It seems to me that it is only when the concept of 'women's reproductive rights' is accepted that we will ever achieve liberation. Without it we can expect that every time a new birth-control method, a new form of technology in relation to birth, a new way of overcoming infertility comes onto the scene, the control over access to and use of it will not be in our hands; and when a new form of technology is seen as threatening enough to the status quo to warrant attention from Parliament, the laws made will not put control over it into women's hands.

(Berer, 1988, p. 24)

Article 2.4 'Detecting genetic diseases: prenatal screening and its problems' by Lynda Birke, Susan Himmelweit and Gail Vines

We decided that we could not, in the course, do justice to the range of new reproductive technologies that were being developed, so we have chosen one which is relatively simple to understand technically and is already used by many women: prenatal screening. However, the political and ethical issues it raises are common to other techniques.

Prenatal screening techniques

Read the first two sections of Article 2.4 (pp. 145–52). This first half of the article describes a range of techniques for prenatal screening and the conditions they detect.

► **ACTIVITY 18** ◄

You do not have to remember the detail but be satisfied that you could explain to a layperson the following techniques, their uses and drawbacks. Complete the following table as a study aid.

Screening techniques	Used to detect	Disadvantages

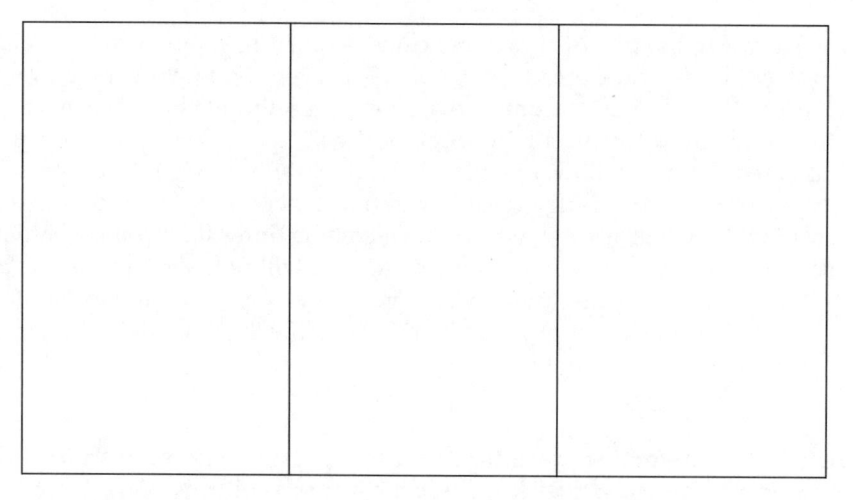

You may like to compare your answer with the one supplied at the end of the Study Guide.

The ethics and politics of screening

Key concepts

screening programmes	genetic counselling
eugenics	selective termination
bio-ethics	choice

Read the rest of Article 2.4 (pp. 152–62). It is here that the ethical debates and the feminist criticism are discussed. You will find the issues discussed wide-ranging and, we hope, stimulating. You will find it beneficial to read it more than once and even to refer back to your Personal Workbook, if you used it earlier, to add those arguments presented by Birke *et al.* with which you have sympathy.

The following are the key issues raised by the article:

- how to assess the effect of screening techniques on different women
- whether screening has medicalized pregnancy even more as well as causing increased anxiety in pregnant women
- whether the use of screening for selective abortion of foetuses is leading to less money being spent on research for a cure for diseases and defects.
- whether screening increases the social stigma of disability
- worries about an underlying eugenics programme – a 'demand for perfect children'
- what a real increase in 'choice' would mean for women
- the ethical debate about what constitute 'trivial' reasons for selective abortion – and the 'abuse' of prenatal screening
- the implications of screening for minority populations and cultures
- the potential for new techniques of detecting genetic disease in embryo using IVF
- the importance of the social and economic context in which children are born.

The development of the concept of reproductive rights is one of the most recent in feminist theory and action. Involved in it are debates about the nature of choice and control. The technology is likely to continue to be developed and used and the feminist position on it is still a contested one.

3
WOMEN PRODUCING SCIENCE AND TECHNOLOGY
(WEEKS 17–19)

3.1 INTRODUCTION

The work associated with your next 'chunk' of study is around the articles in Chapter 3 of *Inventing Women*. We estimate that reading these articles and doing the Study Guide activities suggested should take you *a bit longer than one week*. You have already been introduced to the major theoretical concepts and issues to do with gender and work in Book Two, *Defining Women*, and the Study Guide material associated with it. You have done a great deal of thinking about your own experience of work, but this is likely to be in 'female 'areas of employment (we make that assumption based on the OU student figures quoted in Table 1 earlier) which were also the areas of employment which were the focus of Book Two. The focus of this section is those areas of work which are traditionally male, and if Leibowitz (quoted in Article 2.2) is correct, their invention *created* the original sexual division of labour.

Because of all the publicity surrounding the recruitment of more women into science and technology, in education and employment, it is easy to assume that these fields are simply ones where the traditional ideology of gender has survived longest. And it was assumed that this ideology would change, and that barriers to women's access would inevitably fall. However, it appears that science and technology are more deeply implicated in creating structural gender divisions than most other areas of employment; that they don't just reflect the ideology of gender, they are crucial to determining it. Men in particular see the practice of science or engineering as a symbol of masculinity, and the achievements of these fields are identified as the achievements of *men*. For some men women entering these fields are perceived as a terrible threat not only to gender relations but to masculinity: see Figure 9.

Campus grapples with carnage aftermath

from John Driscoll
MONTREAL

Vigils were held at universities across Canada last week as a shocked nation attempted to come to grips with the massacre of 14 women at the University of Montreal by a man with an intense hatred of women.

Montreal police said that Marc Lepine, 25, walked into a fourth-year mechanical engineering class at the university's Ecole Polytechnique carrying a powerful semi-automatic rifle, separated men and women students, sent the men out of the room and opened fire on the women.

In his pocket he carried a three-page diatribe against "feminists". Mr Lepine's murderous rampage eventually covered three floors of the building and along with killing 14 women, he wounded 12 other women and one man before taking his own life. All but one of the murdered women were engineering students.

Mr Lepin is described as a man recently fired from his job who had experienced problems in his relationships with women. It is believed he once attempted unsuccessfully to enrol as an engineering student.

Examinations at the institute were scheduled to start the day after the massacre but were postponed for four days as a team of psychologists was brought in to assist students and faculty in dealing with the tragedy. Acting director Louis Corville said psychologists have advised students to get back into a regular routine as soon as possible.

A student who survived the murderous rampage called an extraordinary news conference two days later from her hospital bed. Natalie Provost had a bandage over her right temple where a bullet had grazed her and had undergone surgery for bullet wounds to her legs.

She called the news conference, she said, to deliver three messages. First she does not want anyone to feel guilty about what happened. Second, she urged students at the engineering school to pick up their studies, continue their lives and try to forget what happened. Finally, for all women who are thinking about pursuing engineering or any other male-dominated career, "I ask you to envision that possibility with the same enthusiam that you had before what happened."

Figure 9
Source: *Times Higher Education Supplement*, 15 December 1989

Read the Introduction to Chapter 3 of Inventing Women (pp. 162–7).

You will see from this introduction the wide range of material covered in this chapter and the variety of styles in which the material is presented:

- women professional scientists presented through biography
- an historical analysis of the construction of engineering as a profession, from a Marxist perspective
- a case for developing feminist science in education
- a discussion of women in the military
- an analysis of the impact of technology on women's work in the underdeveloped world.

As you study the articles themselves, keep in mind the question: if women were more involved in producing science and technology at the higher levels where power and authority lie, would science and technology be different?

3.2 WOMEN PRACTISING SCIENCE

From the Top

▶ **ACTIVITY 19** ◀

Why not start at the top?
There are three Nobel prizes for science as well as one for peace and one for literature awarded every year. Look at Table 5 which lists fourteen women who have been involved with scientific work that was awarded a prize. How many have you heard of? Look carefully at the column which shows who the prize was awarded to. How many women were not credited in the award?

Women have been involved with the most prestigious work in science in the last hundred years, although their numbers are small. However, they are made to appear even smaller by not always receiving credit for their involvement in the work. You will see that in six cases the women did not receive the award.

You might be interested to know that Jocelyn Bell Burnell is now Professor of Physics at The Open University, and she can also be heard on Radio 04.

Opposition and difference

Why aren't there more women in science and technology? What keeps women out of these fields ? Is it perhaps a lack of interest in, or empathy with, the intellectual or practical endeavours involved; some form of unsuitability, incapability or unpreparedness; protectionism on the part of the professional establishment? One way of exploring these and similar questions is to learn more about the lives and struggles of women who have, with varying degrees of success and recognition, practised as scientists and technologists and we can do this by reading (and writing) biographies.

In the introduction to Chapter 3 of *Inventing Women*, it is suggested that antipathetic attitudes as well as structural barriers hinder women's progress in scientific and technological careers. It is also raises the possibility that successful women scientists practise science differently from their male colleagues.

Turn now to the two biographical articles, 3.1 'Hertha Ayrton : a scientist of spirit' and 3.3 'A feeling for the organism : Fox Keller's life of Barbara McClintock', and read them both with the following questions in mind.

Table 5

Name and profession	Life span	Prize year	Awarded to	Work
Marie Sklodovska Curie French physical chemist	1867–1934	1903 physics	M. Curie, P. Curie and H. Becquerel	radium and polonium discovery
		1911 chemistry	M. Curie	isolation and characterization of radiation as an element
Amalie 'Emmy' Noether German mathematician	1882–1935	1921 physics	A. Einstein	law of photoelectric effect, mathematical physics
Irene Joliot-Curie French physical chemist	1897–1956	1935 chemistry	I. Joliot-Curie F. Joliot-Curie	radioactive isotope synthesis
Hilde Proescholdt Mangold German embryologist	1898–1924	1935 physiology and medicine	H. Spemann	organizer of embryonic development
Lise Meitner Swedish physicist	1878–1968	1944 chemistry	O. Hahn	splitting the atom
Gerty T. Radnitz Cori American biochemist	1896–1957	1947 physiology and medicine	G. Cori, C. Cori and B. Houssay	metabolism of sugar
Chien-Shiung Wu American nuclear physicist	1913–	1957 physics	T. D. Lee and C. N. Yang	disproving the law of conservation of parity
Rosalind E. Franklin English physical chemist	1920–1958	1962 physiology and medicine	J. Watson, F. Crick and M. Wilkins	DNA structure (X-ray diffraction)
Maria Goeppert Mayer theoretical physicist	1906–1972	1963 physics	M. Mayer, J.H.D Jensen and E. P. Wigner	structure of atomic nucleus
Dorothy Crowfoot Hodgkin English biochemist	1910–	1964 chemistry	D. Hodgkin	structure of penicillin, vitamin B-12 etc.
S. Jocelyn Bell Burnell British radioastronomer	1943–	1974 physics	M. Ryle A. Hewish	discovered pulsars
Rosalyn Sussman Yalow American biophysicist	1921–	1977 physiology and medicine	R. Yalow R. Guillemin A. Schally	radioimmunoassay development (with S. Berson)
Barbara McClintock American geneticist	1902–	1983 physiology and medicine	B. McClintock	instability of genes
Rita Levi-Montalcini Italian-American neurobiologist	1909–	1986 physiology and medicine	R. Levi-Montalcini S. Cohen	nerve and epidermal growth factors

Source: *Women Scientists and the Nobel Prize*, Calendar of the Association for Women in Science, Inc. 1988 (Detroit Area Chapter (AWIS-DAC) PO Box 721072, Berkley, Michigan 48072

What evidence is there in these accounts of the lives and work of Hertha Ayrton and Barbara McClintock which you could use to support the antipathy and structural barrier arguments ?

Did their backgrounds (family, education, work environment) help them to pursue their scientific work?

How was their work (their fields, their careers, their contributions) affected by their being women?

Is there anything in theses accounts to support the view that women do things differently, that there may be a 'women's science'?

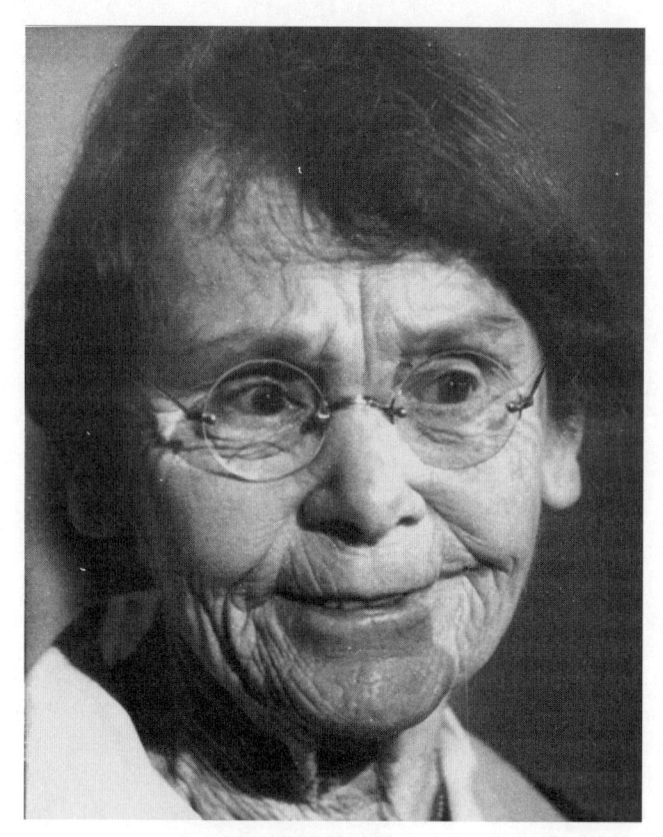

Figure 10
Barbara McClintock in 1981

Although short, Mason's account of Hertha Ayrton's life does give us a fairly comprehensive picture. We know something of her education, how she became involved in science and how it influenced her life. We also learn how she managed her roles as wife, mother and daughter while also becoming a successful scientist. Note the enabling support, especially financial, which she received from other women. Ayrton's scientific interests and achievements are detailed and her relationships with the scientific community are explored. The antipathy she encountered is also well illustrated. Armstrong's views are particularly ironic as he is lauded as the founder of modern science education in Britain.

The article about McClintock doesn't give such a broad picture but that is because it is an examination of extracts from a book-length biography. From this we know very little about where she came from – her background, education, scientific aspirations or anything else about her. What sort of barriers did she have to overcome? We would need to go back to the Fox Keller book to start exploring those questions. The extracts you read have been chosen to highlight a particular view of science as practised by McClintock. Or at least Fox Keller's conception of McClintock's science.

► **ACTIVITY 20** ◄

At the start of their chapter about McClintock, Kirkup and Smith Keller make the point that a biography is 'a reconstruction [of a person's life and work] viewed through a particular lens'. Look again at these two articles. What strikes you about the views presented by the biographers here? Will identifying a view or the purpose of a biographer affect the weight you attach to their evidence and arguments?

COMMENT

Note the final section in the article about McClintock – 'McClintock's vision or Fox Keller's?'. Perhaps we need to know as much about Fox Keller as she is telling us about McClintock before we can can consider whether what we have learned about McClintock's practice of science supports the notion that women's science is or could be different.

Mason wants us to be very aware of the details of Ayrton's scientific contribution and about the barriers she encountered in her attempts to be a full member of the existing scientific establishment. Indeed the story is structured around the unsuccessful proposal for her admission as a Fellow of the Royal Society. But notice how much space and weight she also gives to Ayrton's involvement with feminism and the suffrage movement, to the opening up of higher education opportunities for women and to the networks of support that women offer to one another.

Using scientific biography

In an article about scientific biography, in which she uses *Hypatia's Heritage* as an example, Tomaselli explores the contribution biography can make to feminism. First of all it can inform and countermand attitudes which exclude women from a culture and, in this case, suggest they are incapable of scientific creativity. It can also kindle interest and generate more thought and research providing a greater wealth of role models . It might also contribute eventually to women's ability to '... imagine ways in which the pursuit of scientific research could be adapted to meet the needs of wives and mothers who are not always free to run to the lab. at every hour of the day and night.'

What do we need to know in accounts of women scientists?

We need to know not only about their science and how they came to do it and their achievements and impact but also about their circumstances, their family life, their education, their class and financial means, their friends, their professional relationships – indeed their life taken as a whole and related to the total historical context.

> Much as it will benefit our knowledge of what individual women scientists actually did and how they did it, scientific biography may well also obscure or diminish in importance women's place in science. Science isn't produced in a social, economic or political vacuum. It is part and parcel of life in civil society which the labour and culture of women sustain. Women aren't only its objects. They are its makers in a sense which transcends the sum total of the participation of individual women in science or high culture. They produce it in countless, albeit anonymous, ways. They are moreover also its readers, popularizers and teachers.
>
> *(Tomaselli, 1991, p. 105)*

In the light of those comments, read the following extracts from biographical sketches of Lise Meitner and Rosalind Franklin.

Figure 11
Lise Meitner, with Otto Hahn

The atomic bomb was made possible by a pacifist Jew working in Berlin in the 1930s. Had she known to what uses her discovery of nuclear fission (it was she who coined the term) would be put, Dr Lise Meitner might never have begun her research. As it was, she retired from the field of atomic physics as soon as the city of Hiroshima was destroyed. 'It was an unfortunate accident that this discovery came about in time to war', Meitner said. 'I myself have not worked on smashing the atom with the idea of producing death-dealing weapons. Women have a great responsibility, and they are obliged to try so far as they can to prevent another war.'

Lise Meitner was born in 1878 in Vienna, to a large Jewish family – although she and her seven siblings were baptised and raised as Protestants, probably to protect them from rampant anti-Semitism. As a youngster, Lise was fascinated by the work of Marie Curie, and entered the University of Vienna in 1901 determined to study the new science of physics, even though such work by a female was discouraged and laughed at. When she received her doctorate from that institution in 1906, she became one of the first women to do so.

... [She then moved to Berlin and studied under] Dr Max Planck, who would win the Nobel Prize for his theory of quantum mechanics. Lise was Planck's assistant for three of his most productive years.

While she worked with Dr Planck Lise met Dr Otto Hahn, who would become her lifelong collaborator. Since Emil Fischer would allow no women in his Chemical Institute, Meitner and Hahn set up a research lab in a carpenter's workshop, which they equipped to measure radiation and conduct experiments in the formation of new elements.

The First World War created a break in Dr Meitner's work: she enlisted in the Austrian Army as a nurse and radiographer ...

The status of women changed abruptly during World War I, since those who took up positions of responsibility by necessity proved they also could compete by choice. In 1918 Dr Meitner was appointed head of the physics department at the prestigious Kaiser Wilhelm Institute and was asked to organize a division to study radioactivity. In 1926 she became a full professor of physics at the University of Berlin, where she continued to study the correlation between gamma and beta rays ...

... While bombarding uranium with slow-speed neutrons, the scientists were amazed to detect the presence of barium in the final product, a lighter-than-uranium element that had no evident reason to be there. Lise Meitner and Otto Hahn had just split the atom, although neither of them realized it at the time.

Just as Lise's experiments were coming to a head, so was the power of the Nazi Party. Even though she was never a practising Jew, neither did she keep her birthright a secret. She was summarily dismissed from her position at the University of Berlin, and – now that the Nazis had absorbed Austria – her foreign citizenship was no protection. She had to flee for her life.

Only Dr Hahn knew that Lise's 'vacation' in Holland was a cover for a prearranged exodus to Sweden. Lise got to Holland with the help of friends, and she slipped across the North Sea to Denmark barely ahead of Nazi patrol boats. In Copenhagen she stayed with physicist Niels Bohr and his wife.

Safely in Stockholm, working at the new Nobel Institute for Physics, Meitner published an earthshaking paper. She and her nephew Otto Frisch were duplicating some of Otto Hahn's experiments when Lise realized the significance of splitting the nucleus of an uranium atom. She calculated the potential release of energy in such an event, using Einstein's equation $E = mc^2$, and told the world that the nucleus of a uranium atom could release twenty million times more energy than exploding an equal amount of TNT. The nuclear age began – for better or worse – when Dr Meitner published her findings in the British journal *Nature* on January 16, 1939.

Immediately after the publication of Dr Meitner's study, the world powers raced to convert this source of energy into a destructive weapon. Dr Meitner had no interest in turning her 'Promised Land of atomic energy' into a bomb. Invited to work on the Manhattan Project, she refused and said that she hoped the weapon project would fail. Two days after the bomb was dropped on Hiroshima, Dr Meitner had a conversation with First Lady Eleanor Roosevelt. 'I hope', said Dr Meitner, 'that it will be possible to ... prevent such horrible things as we have had to live through.' ...

Lise Meitner ... died in a nursing home in England on October 27, 1968, only a few days before her ninetieth birthday. Dr Otto Hahn, her co-worker of thirty years, had died three months earlier. She never accepted or approved of the uses to which her discovery was put, and she never received the Nobel Prize for her breakthrough, an honour that Hahn received in 1944.

(Vare and Ptacek, 1987, pp. 148–52)

■ ■ ■

Microchemist Rosalind Franklin went through her scientific life with a chip on her shoulder, and it's no wonder. Even though she was the first researcher to discern the complex structure of the DNA (deoxyribonucleic acid) molecule, her colleagues wouldn't so much as let her in their meetings to discuss her findings. Instead, they cavalierly took her papers and handed them around to her competition. After all, Miss Franklin was invading an all-male scientific establishment and to complicate matters, she was Jewish.

It was Rosalind Franklin who was the integral fourth team member – with Maurice Wilkins, James Watson, and Francis Crick – responsible for the discovery of the famed 'double helix'. [They received the Nobel prize in 1962 but] Franklin died of cancer in 1958, and the Nobel Prize goes only to living people. That her contributions continued to be denigrated by her colleagues (James Watson referred to her as 'Rosy' in his 1968 book *The Double Helix* and implied that she was little more than a lab. assistant) is shameful. In fact, Rosalind Franklin was the first person, back in 1951, to deduce the helical structure of DNA; she even showed Watson the fundamental error in his first double-helix model and put him on the track to his prizewinning findings.

... Born in 1920 into a socially prominent Jewish banking family in London, she disappointed her parents by heading for a scientific career instead of a philanthropical one. When she graduated from Newnham College at Cambridge in 1941, she was awarded a research scholarship to work under Ronald Norrish (who would win the Nobel Prize himself in 1967) – a man who resented her very presence and fought her every step of the way. Franklin relocated to the Central Laboratory of Chemical Sciences in Paris, where she made important discoveries in crystallography and molecular structure, and returned to work at King's College in London. There she again found herself supervised by a scientist who considered her an affront. Maurice Wilkins refused to accept female doctoral candidates under his direction as late as the 1970s, and between 1951 and 1953 he was known to have turned Franklin's findings – without her permission – over to his friends Watson and Crick.

Although she published a breakthrough paper on the structure of DNA in 1953, and although her X-ray photographs were used by Watson as vital evidence in his grant application, Franklin became so frustrated with the treatment she was receiving that she left King's College in 1953. She took a research position at Birkbeck College instead, where she delineated important findings about virus particles. While at Birkbeck, she was forbidden to talk about DNA, although her work in virology contributed significantly to the understanding of genetics. She mounted an exhibition at the 1958 World's Fair in Brussels at the behest of the Royal Society, but this official recognition was both too little and too late. In that same year, she learned she had incurable cancer.

Always a loner, Franklin told none of her co-workers that she was in pain; she asked for no sympathy, and she received none. She continued to work until her death at age thirty-seven, dying a bitter and frustrated woman.

(Vare and Ptacek, 1987, pp. 214–16)

▶ **ACTIVITY 21** ◀

What particular aspects of their lives would you want to explore before using them as examples to support a particular argument? What, if anything, can you surmise about the purpose of the biographers here?

COMMENT

Both these biographical sketches come from a book called *Mothers of Invention* and subtitled 'Forgotten women and their unforgettable ideas'. The main emphasis throughout the book is on the achievements and lack of recognition of the women portrayed. Meitner and Franklin fall into the group of women you identified in Activity 18 as being involved with Nobel prize-winning work but being uncredited in the award.

Meitner came from a cultural background – middle-European Jewish – which at that period gave the world many successful, innovative scientists. I would want to look more closely at the influence her family and friends had on her career. Her relationship with, and responsibility for, the outcomes of her work strike me as a particular thing the biographers here would like to draw attention to as an issue worth exploring.

The Franklin sketch is very brief and quite different in tone. It could hardly be said to be in praise of famous women! I find it judgemental of the behaviour of both Franklin and her colleagues in different ways, without giving enough evidence to support those judgements.

GRIMBLEDON DOWN   Bill Tidy

3.3 WOMEN SCIENTISTS IN THE MAKING?

One of the influences in the lives of successful women scientists must be education and, in particular, access to stimulating science education. For decades it was held to be inappropriate to include science, except of the domestic variety and perhaps a little nature study, in the curriculum for girls in school. When this pattern began to change, opportunities in girls' schools for the study of the physical sciences was limited by lack of facilities and lack of specialist teachers. In mixed schools girls are often excluded from practical and investigative work and lose interest. For all sorts of reasons and circumstances girls have been under-represented in science education and the logical consequence of this is that there are very few women in science and technology based employment.

Over the last decade there have been many changes and in principle, with the introduction of the National Curriculum in England and Wales, everyone will study some science until the age of sixteen. Whitelegg explores some of these changes in Article 3.3. What are your recollections of studying science at school – if indeed you did ? If you have contact with children and young people currently studying science and technology (also a National Curriculum subject), you will have some idea about how different it is now.

▶ **ACTIVITY 22** ◀

Entries for public examinations is a fairly popular measure of the proportion of girls participating in science education. Look at Figure 12 which shows physics entries for school exams in England and Wales over a period of years. Since the school populations of boys and girls are roughly equal, it illustrates the marked difference in the popularity (or is it availability?) of physics with boys and girls.

Calculate the *percentage* increase in the number of candidates in each category over the period 1968–1982. (Note that this is not the start date of the graph.)

Write a short paragraph describing any trends in physics education for girls which you think can be shown from this graph and speculate on reasons for these trends.

Answers to the statistical questions will be found at the end of the Study Guide.

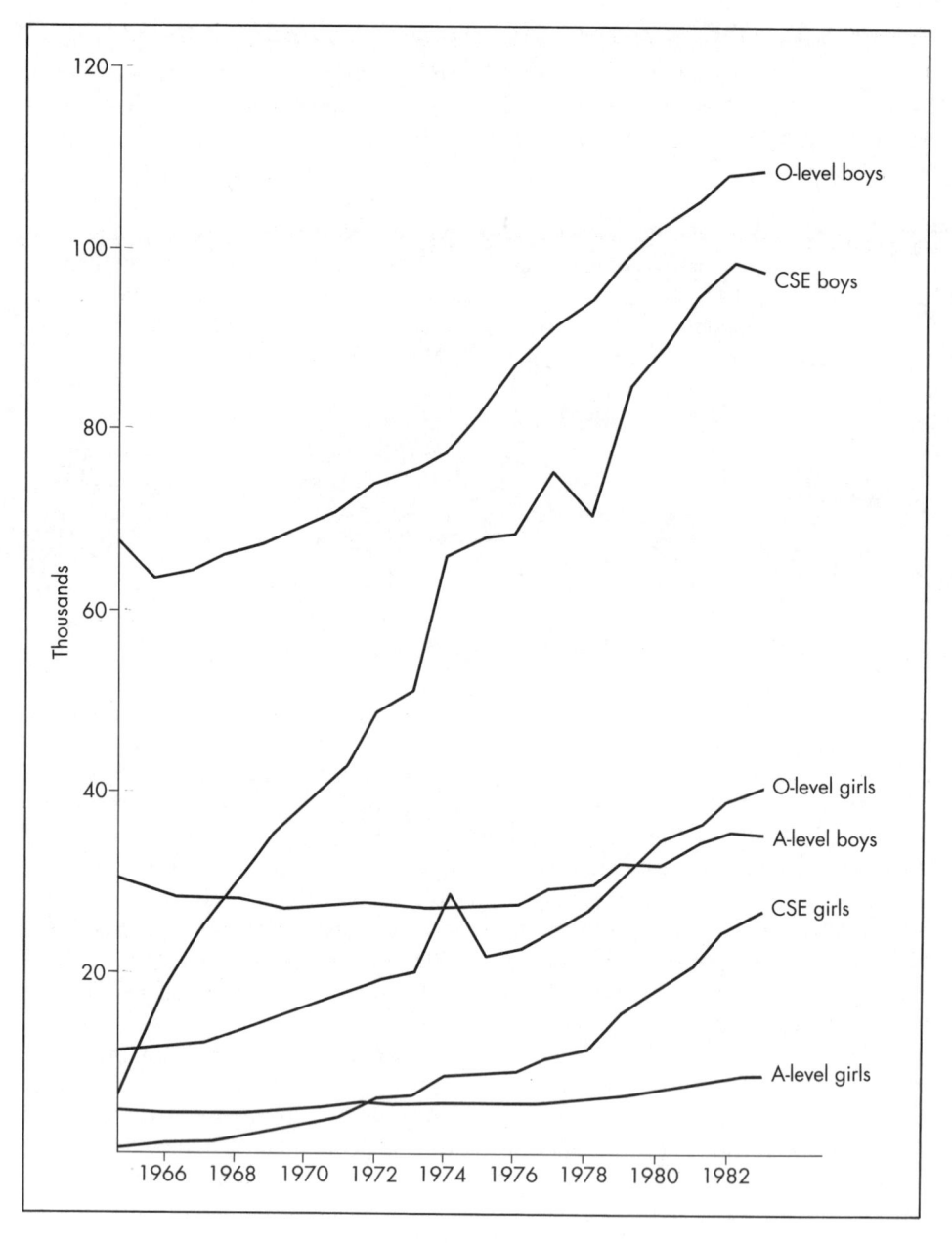

Figure 12
Physics entries for school exams, by sex

COMMENT

From 1968 to 1978 there is a steady rise in the numbers of girls taking both O-level and CSE (ignoring the sharp blip in O-level in 1974). From 1978 onwards the rise is steeper. As the figures are in actual numbers of entries, the general rise could be because school populations were rising but the steeper rise from 1978 onwards may be due to interventions. Girls were being encouraged into science. In particular they were being shown, before they made exam choices, that by not getting science qualifications they were ruling themselves out of a wide variety of career choices.

Until the mid 1970s there was little change in A-level. After that, entries began to increase, possibly because more girls were taking physics up to O-level and so there was a larger pool of potential candidates.

Note that the percentage increase in the number of girl candidates in this period is much greater than that for boys in all three exams.

Article 3.2 'Girls in science education: of rice and fruit trees' by Liz Whitelegg

In Article 3.2 Liz Whitelegg assesses in particular the potential impact of the National Curriculum on science and technology education for girls. The National Curriculum for England and Wales came onto the statute book in 1989 and all maintained schools are obliged to provide a basic curriculum of ten compulsory foundation subjects for all pupils. Within this curriculum three subjects – mathematics, language and science – are designated as core subjects. Technology is one of the other foundation subjects. The compulsory education range (5–16) is divided into four key stages and the content, learning and assessment of the curriculum are related to these stages. Each curriculum area is specified in terms of attainment targets and levels of attainment within those attainment targets are related to the key stages. Programmes of study outline what needs to be taught but do not constrain teachers in the way they teach it and, as Whitelegg points out, the National Curriculum does not specifically address the issue of equal opportunity.

> Now turn to Article 3.2 and read Whitelegg's discussion about the current state of science education for girls. As you read, make notes on the following.
>
> How are gender inequalities apparent and how are they reinforced in the classroom?
>
> What factors does Whitelegg suggest might negate the intent of the National Curriculum to ensure that girls do study science?
>
> How might science and science teaching be reconstructed?

Whitelegg describes some of the effects of gender stereotyping and of children's different self-images and socialization. Girls and boys exhibit differences in their concerns and interests when carrying out science or technology tasks. Look at Figure 13 which shows typical responses to the task of designing a new vehicle and note the marked differences between the girls' and boys' designs. Similarly when asked to design a pram, girls and boys differed in their design purpose. The girls were concerned to improve the safety of the vehicle using different-shaped wheels etc. The boys computerized their pram so the baby could be transported without the aid of an adult. These differences are often not picked up by teachers and typically the girls' views of relevance tend to go unrecognized.

Whitelegg highlights concerns relating to the promotion of spatial ability in girls (remember the discussion by Birke in Article 2.1), the importance of appropriate contexts for learning and problems of gender-linked differences in test performance. All these are echoed in a recent report on design and technology education: see Figure 14.

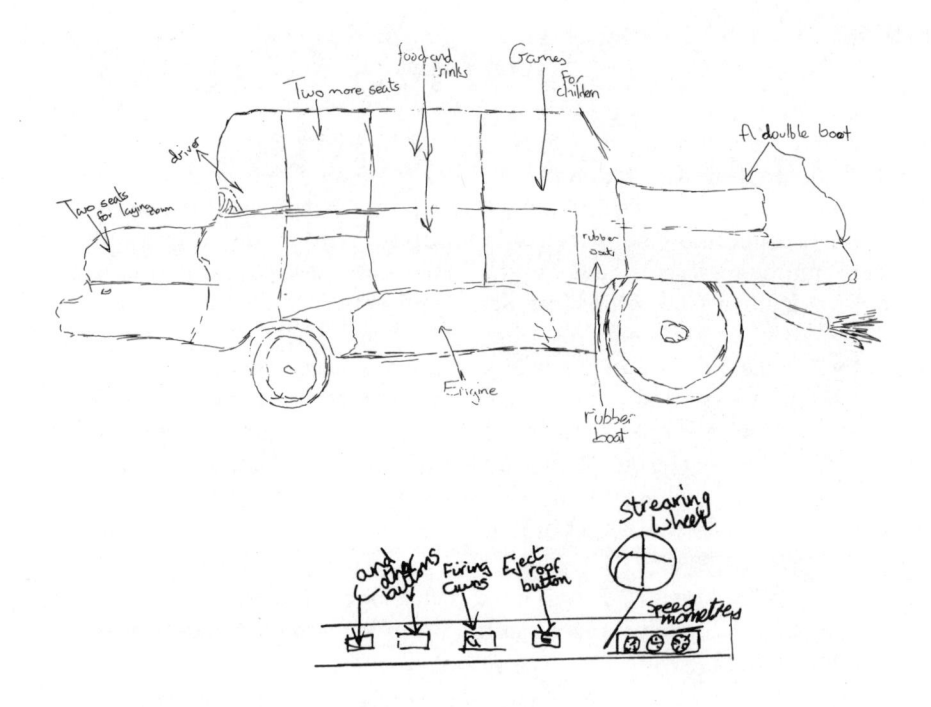

(a) Girls' typical design

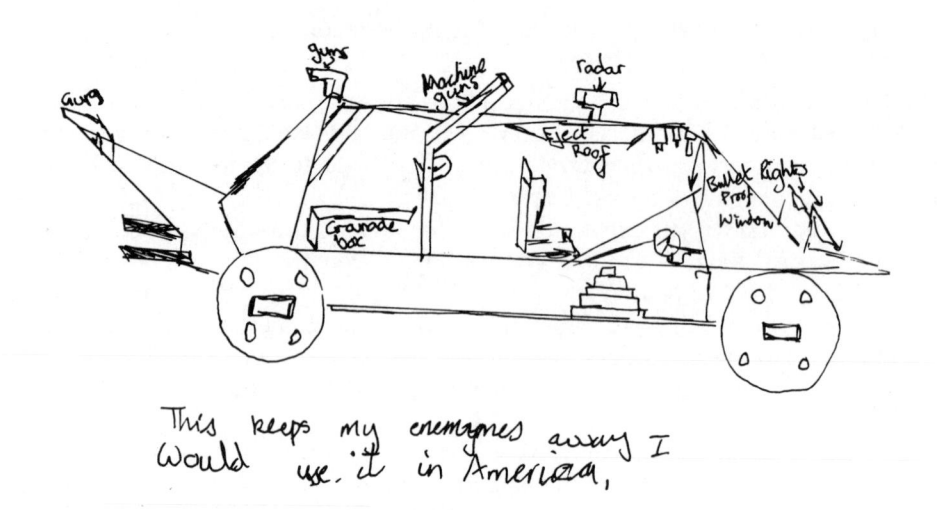

(b) Boys' typical design

Figure 13

New exams could hold back girls

Girls: flexing that all-important spatial ability.

Changes to National Curriculum testing as dictated by the Department of Education and Science (DES) could have disastrous effects on the future percentage of women in science, design and technology related subjects.

The DES/School Examinations and Assessment Council's (SEAC) new specifications for testing pupils envisage short, written, de-contextualised tests. But a new study on *The Assessment of Performance in Design and Technology*, published by the SEAC, reveals that girls fare better in design and technology related subjects when tests are contextualised and personalised.

Richard Kimbell, principal author of the report, says that the new system may well affect the performance of girls in design-related studies, and further deter them from undertaking them.

The SEAC findings are based on a study of nearly 10,000 15-year-olds from a representative number of 700 schools, stratified by type, region and size. The sample was also enriched in certain tests to include 'target' pupils, known to be studying specified design and technological courses.

Tests on the students aimed to find out what processes were involved in design and technology and what procedures produced better results among pupils.

Results revealed that girls overall fared better than boys when the design/technology tasks were put to them within a context, when the way the tasks were presented enabled the students to identify with the tasks.

'Generally speaking,' said Kimbell, 'When the girls fail in science it is because they don't personalise the task. If this is presented to them in a context that relates to people and the real world, they come through with flying colours.

'Boys appear more ready to take tasks on trust and get on with it, even if they don't quite see why they are doing it. The problem is that too often scientific subjects have been taught in an impersonal, de-contextualised way, and this has a more serious effect on girls than on boys.'

Other results of the study reveal that girls fare better when presented with open tasks (improving products or systems for gardens or gardeners) and tight procedures for tackling the task (evaluate strengths and weaknesses of your approach).

Boys fare better when presented with a tightly defined task (create a bird-scaring device that spins in the wind) and with loose procedures (getting on with the job using free modelling, discussion).

The results could have important consequences for the education process. 'You have to look at the training programme you put your students through in the light of these results,' said Kimbell. 'If you tend to use the same procedure all the time, for example, closed tasks with open procedures, pupils that do well will always do well. You need to make sure that the tasks presented in a course represent a whole variety of approaches and procedures so that different students get used to coping in a variety of situations'.

Conclusions on the essence of the design and technology process were also reached by the study. These reveal that it involves both active and reflective processes. Ideas can be better developed when there is interaction of mind and hand.

When students were asked to develop ideas through interaction of speculation (mind) with modelling (hand), results were higher than those where pupils had used only models or only speculation.

'If you start out with a hazy idea with a solution in mind, if you don't do something practical with it you can't develop the idea,' said Kimbell. 'The act of expression helps you to understand and develop the idea. This is why the concept of technology as being just about doing things is wrong. It is about doing things in relation to the thinking behind them.'

The SEAC project was originally commissioned by the DES/Assessment of Performance Unit to assess capability in technology. Kimbell is director of the Technology Education Research Unit at Goldsmiths' College, University of London. The college is soon to run conferences and publish material for teachers on the subject.

Figure 14
Source: *Architects' Journal*, 6 November 1991

ACTIVITY 23

Things don't improve as we move up the education pyramid. Look at the data for the general divide in subjects studied by full time undergraduates in 1990 in Figure 15.

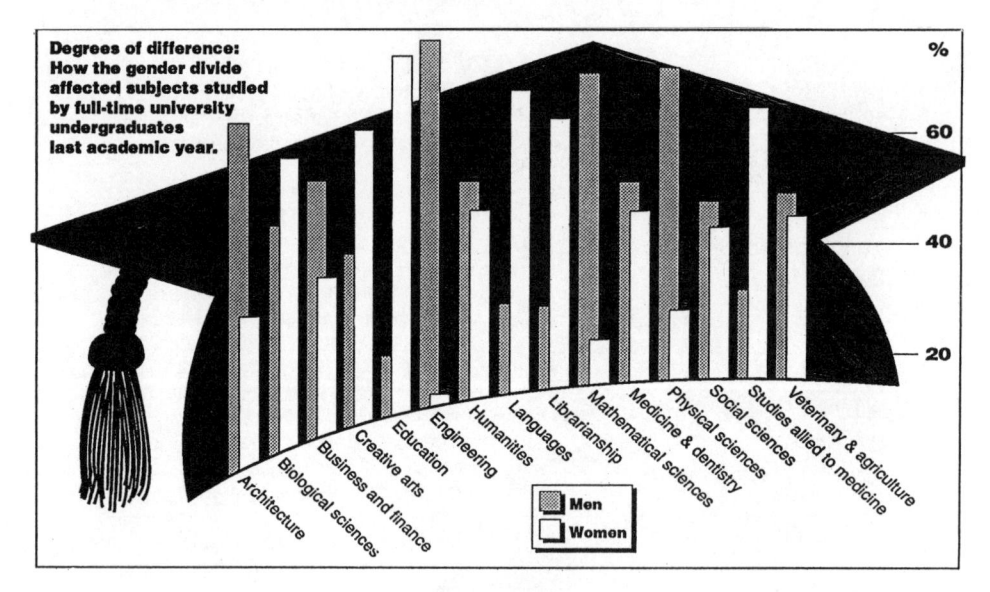

Degrees of difference: How the gender divide affected subjects studied by full-time university undergraduates last academic year.

Figure 15
Subjects studied by full-time university undergraduates, 1990–91, by sex

(a) Which subject had the smallest proportion of women students?

(b) How do mathematical sciences and physical sciences fare?

(c) Pick out those subjects which are roughly 50/50.

(d) Compare studies 'Allied to medicine' with 'Medicine and dentistry'.

(e) Can you compare the data in this figure with those for 1985/86 given in section 1.1?

COMMENT

Engineering has the smallest percentage of women followed by mathematical science and physical science. Medicine and dentistry, veterinary and agriculture and the humanities are about 50/50 but in studies allied to medicine women outnumber men by 2:1.

Did you have any difficulty interpreting this data? I hope you weren't put off by the curve of the mortar board. This has been superimposed onto the chart for visual effect and the bottom portion isn't shown.

You can extend the scale on the right-hand side and put in the base line. (The left-hand side of the men architects is on the base line.)

While the two sets of data (Figure 15 and Figure 3) are referring to the same thing – the numbers of men and women studying certain subject areas – it is not possible to make direct comparisons because the subjects have been grouped differently and defined rather vaguely.

Why do girls need science education?

Intervention to try and encourage more girls to continue the study of science is not only about allowing the development of potential for an individual or the removal of stereotyping and its resultant restriction of liberty. It is important to keep in mind the importance of science education and of scientific and technological 'literacy' in life these days.

3.4 WOMEN IN ENGINEERING

You do not need to do a women's studies course to know that women do not tend to work as professional engineers or as skilled 'craftsmen'. But did you realize just how small that involvement presently is?

► **ACTIVITY 24** ◄

Look at Table 6. It is only an estimate but it is probably the best guide you can find to the distribution of women workers in the engineering industry at the end of the 1980s. Extract the following information from the figures:

(a) What jobs in the engineering industry are women most likely to be found in?

(b) Which jobs have the highest proportion of women and which the lowest?

Table 6 British Engineering Industry: estimated number of employees, analysed by occupational category and sex, April 1989

Occupation	Male	Female	Total
Managerial staff	121,840	6,604	128,444
Professional engineers, scientists and technologists	88,452	4,858	93,310
Technicians and technician engineers, including draughtsmen	161,463	5,869	167,7332
Administrative and professional staff	103,109	27,482	130,591
Clerks, office machine operators, secretaries and typist	41,863	132,372	174,235
Supervisors	80,068	8218	88,286
Craftsmen in occupations normally entered by apprenticeship	311,649	2,908	314,557
Operators and other employees (excluding canteen staff)	586,146	198,954	795,100
Totals	1,504,590	387,265	1,891,855

Note: Slight discrepancies may exist because of rounding.
Source: Engineering Industry Training Board, *Annual Report 1989/90*, EITB Publications, Watford, 1990

Most people find figures of this magnitude difficult to conceptualize. There are two techniques which will help you. The first is to calculate what percentage of each category are women, and/or what percentage of all women are in each category, and the second is to sketch the data as a bar chart to have a visual impression of it.

Please try to do this yourself and then check your own work against that given at the end of the Study Guide.

COMMENT

The largest number of women working in the engineering industry are working as operators, followed by those working as clerks and office workers; the smallest number are working as 'craftsmen' followed by professional engineers. When you calculate women as a percentage of each category you find that the situation looks slightly different. Women are 76 per cent of clerks and office workers and only 25 per cent of operators; they are less than 1 per cent of craftsmen, and only 3.5 per cent of technicians and 5 per cent of professional engineers. If you take the total number of women working in the engineering industry, just over half of them are working as operators and another one-third are working as clerks and office workers. It will have been no surprise for you to find that women are overwhelmingly concentrated in the lower paid, lower skilled occupations.

The question is: how did it get like this and how easy is it to change?

3.5 TECHNOLOGY, PRODUCTION AND POWER

Article 3.4 'Technology, production and power' by Cynthia Cockburn

Article 3.4 is an attempt to theorize how this situation came about. Cynthia Cockburn is well-known for her detailed historical analyses of the gendering of particular British industries. The piece we have chosen is from her 1985 book, *Machinery of Dominance: women, men and technical know-how*, where she looks at the way different areas of the production process are gendered. Here she uses a Marxist historical analysis to explain the creation of 'engineering' as a male area of work.

Key concepts

industrialization	transferable knowledge
power	materialist understanding of history
class society	private and public
capitalism	waged work
means of production	organization of labour

(You will have met many of these already in your study of Book Two.)

> Read the first four sections of Article 3.4 (pp. 196–205), stopping before the section entitled 'Women's relationship to the machine'. These sections deal with men's relationship to the technology of production, from pre-history to the end of the nineteenth century. As you read, make notes on the following.
>
> What does Cockburn mean by a 'materialist understanding of history'?
>
> Cockburn's historical model of the change from peasant society to capitalist society is very explicit about how that change affected skilled male workers, with respect to their social relationships with other classes and with respect to their skills. Summarize this in your own words.
>
> What was similar and what was different about the craft guilds of the Middle Ages and the trades unions of the nineteenth century?
>
> What was women's involvement with the technology of production before capitalism and industrialization?
>
> Then read the rest of the article (pp. 205–11) and makes notes on:
>
> - the advantages and disadvantages to women of industrialization
> - the kinds of work that women were doing in the nineteenth-century factory
> - men's response to women working in industry
> - the effect of the two Great Wars of the twentieth century on women's industrial work.
>
> Notice that Cockburn ends with a speculation and a question about what might happen to women's industrial employment in the rest of this century? What is her underlying worry?

By a materialist understanding of history Cockburn means one in which the focus of study is not individuals and their actions but social processes, and in particular those processes which produce the economic and technological basis of society. This kind of study of history can be as effective at making the contribution of women invisible as can the study of 'famous men', unless women are explicitly a focus. In Cockburn's Marxist model, what drives class-structured societies is a struggle for access to the surplus (food, wealth etc.) generated by society, and the outcome of this is often warfare.

Cockburn sees women historically as primarily involved in those productive activities that are associated with domestic consumption, leaving men to be iron workers and tool makers. As metal working was used for the production of arms, and warfare was basically a masculine activity, this was the prime reason why metal working became a male activity. In peasant societies people (i.e. families *not* individuals) owned not only their skills but the tools of their trade. In capitalist societies, where manufacture is centralized in large factories, the machinery (the means of production) is owned by the capitalist. The skilled person owns only their own skills. Capitalism produced new classes: the wealthy capitalists, the skilled engineers or mechanics who functioned as middle men servicing the machines, and the semi-skilled or unskilled operators who used them. Skills were deconstructed into a series of unskilled tasks that required the minimum of training to carry out, and for which people could be paid less.

Both the craft guild and the trades unions were organizations of workers which existed primarily to control access to skills and to provide a more powerful base to negotiate with those who bought the skills. They were both male organizations that deliberately excluded women. Cockburn suggests that as far as the guilds were concerned women were not seen as a threat to male employment. The nineteenth-century unions did see women as a threat to male employment and therefore their strategies for excluding women were much stronger.

Although women were exploited by early industrialization because they were not organized through trades unions, they also received benefits from it. For many women it was their first opportunity to work outside the domestic environment and to earn an independent wage. They worked in the unskilled and semi-skilled areas of production, preparing raw materials, finishing and packing final products and on routine operating/production tasks. The response of masculine unions was to see women as competition, and to fight this by denying them access to skills and union membership. In the UK the two Great Wars provided the opportunity for the first time for women to demonstrate that they could acquire and practise those technical skills which had for so long been restricted to men.

Cockburn ends by arguing that if economics is the main driving force of society then we should see the sexual divisions of work breaking down even further in the recession of the late 1980s/early 1990s, as women become more attractive to employ than men. If we do not see this, she suggests we should be investigating what the other driving forces of society are.

► **ACTIVITY 25** ◄

Look at Figure 16. It shows changes in numbers of men and women in employment in selected occupational groups between 1979 and 1989.

Have women and men gained and lost jobs roughly equitably?

Where have women lost most and where have they gained most and how does this compare with men?

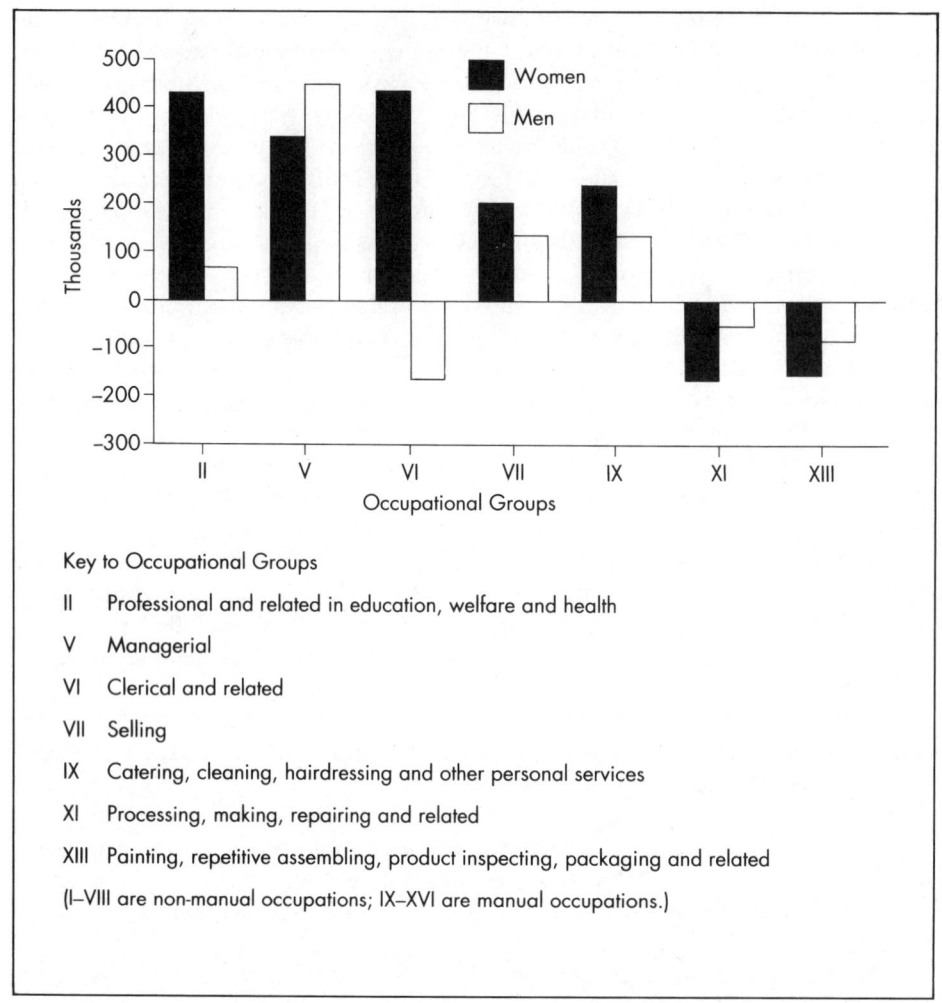

(a) Persons in employment, selected occupations, changes 1979–89, Great Britain

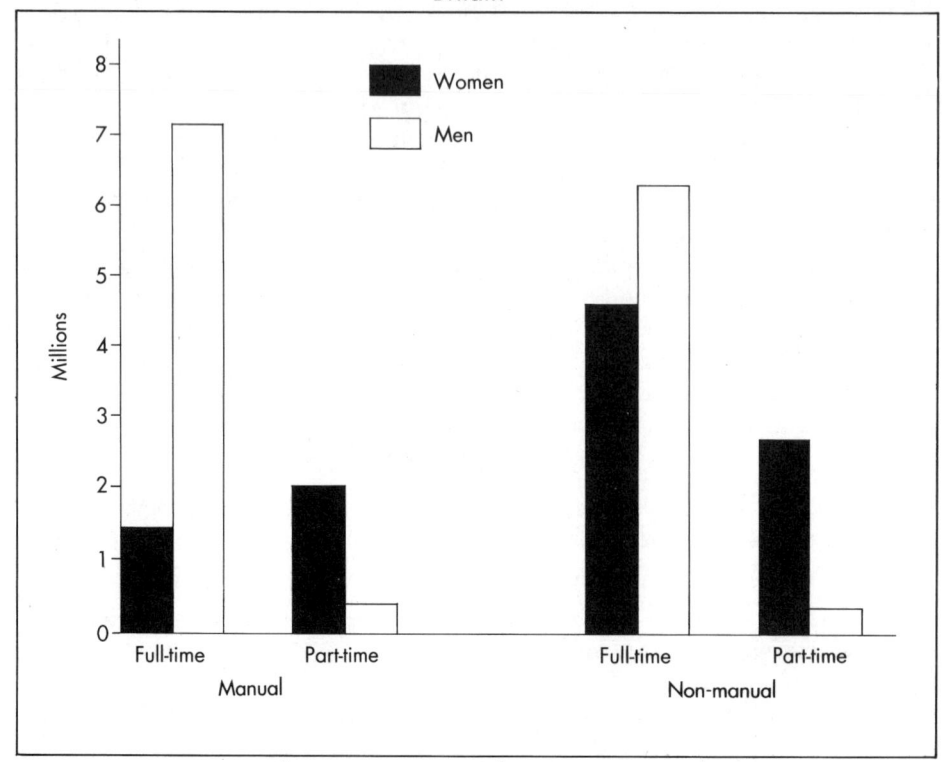

Key to Occupational Groups

II   Professional and related in education, welfare and health
V   Managerial
VI   Clerical and related
VII Selling
IX   Catering, cleaning, hairdressing and other personal services
XI   Processing, making, repairing and related
XIII Painting, repetitive assembling, product inspecting, packaging and related

(I–VIII are non-manual occupations; IX–XVI are manual occupations.)

(b) Persons in employment, 1989

Figure 16

Source: Labour Force Survey, from EOC, 1991

COMMENT

In the occupations shown in Figure 16 there has been a much greater increase in women's employment than in men's, although in general where an occupation has had an increase in workers there has been an increase in both men and women; the exception is clerical work where male jobs have been lost while female jobs have expanded. This has happened during a period when office technology has been revolutionized by computers, and the outcome would support Cockburn's expectation of capitalism's flexibility. In processing and assembling, where women were already under-represented (for example, in 1987 women were 36 per cent of workers in making and repairing jobs, and 46 per cent of workers in painting, assembling and packaging), a much higher proportion of women's jobs has been lost. This suggests that in these older industries men have defended their positions to the detriment of female employment during a period of recession, and that the ideology of gender has been stronger than capitalist economic forces in these traditional occupations.

3.6 THE TECHNOLOGY OF WARFARE

Although a number of authors that you have studied in this part of the course have stressed the importance of warfare in the development of technology and of a gendered society, this does not mean that women have had no participation in designing and using weapons. Their involvement may have been small but, because warfare is viewed as an archetypal masculine activity, even that has been rendered invisible. Women scientists, for example, were involved in the design of nuclear weapons; Lise Meitner has already been mentioned, but there were others: Maria Goeppert-Mayer was a member of the team which isolated uranium-235, Leona Libby was a member of the Manhattan Project which built the first atomic bomb, Marguerite Chang designed the trigger mechanism for underground nuclear testing. At the least prestigious end of warfare are the women who have historically functioned as support services to the military: cooks, nurses, wives and even foot soldiers, discussed by Julie Wheelwright in her book *Amazons and Military Maids* (1989).

In Article 3.6 and Radio 07 Julie Wheelwright explores the role of women in the military in the 1990s, both in modern high technology forces and in liberation armies. The radio programme is concerned with the effect of gender ideology and sex discrimination on the women soldiers themselves. The article is concerned with how the modern military is responding to developments in technology and in equal opportunities legislation.

▶ ACTIVITY 26 ◀

Look at Map 4, Military service, in the colour plate section of Book Three and at the different pictograms which illustrate women's role in the military worldwide. What can you discover about women's role in the armed forces and their variations between countries?

COMMENT

Women's involvement in masculine activities is greatest during war-time, as Cockburn demonstrated with engineering. It is no surprise to find that in the UK women's numbers in the armed forces were greatest between 1939 and 1946, when they reached almost 10 per cent of the total of the armed forces, and nearly half a million British women were soldiers. Unfortunately the pictograms are dramatically out of scale, representing 10 per cent visually as more than a quarter of the 'pie'.

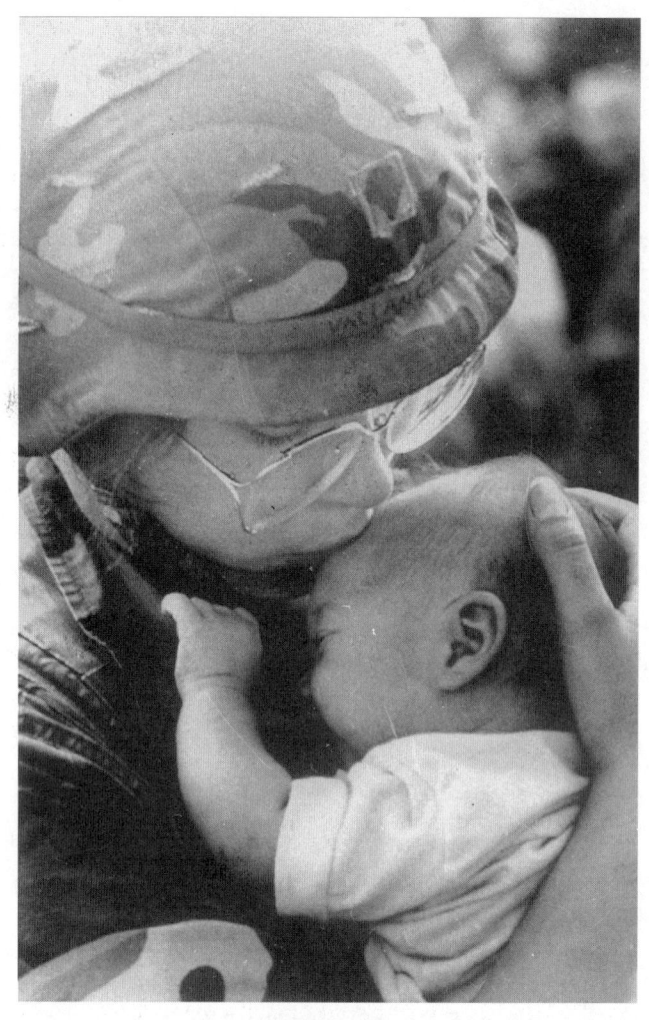

Figure 17
Tender troops: an American medic says goodbye to her seven-week-old baby daughter before leaving for the Gulf War, August 1990

The 'tin hat' pictogram on the opposite page shows that by the 1980s women were 5 per cent of the UK armed forces, a much higher proportion than in the rest of Europe but lower than in the USA and Canada. You might have found the list of countries where women have been combatants in revolutionary armies surprising both in terms of their numbers and some of the countries included, such as Iran where civilian life exhibits strong gender divisions. If you look at the central map you will see that accurate information about the role of women in the military is unavailable for more countries than it is available for. However, the dark brown areas of the map show how few countries *definitely include* women in all roles. In many of the others where they are in the military, women are excluded from combat.

Women's involvement in the military remains an area of controversy amongst feminists. British feminists have tended to be hostile to the military and to identify it as a purely masculine activity and one of the supporting edifices of capitalism, imperialism and patriarchy. The function of the military is different in other countries and the response of women to it is different:

> It is generally true that military service brings social and economic benefits; by excluding women from service, they are excluded from these benefits too. In many countries, the military is the government – which means that the government is exclusively male and women are held at a great distance from power.

(Seager and Olson, 1986, p. 116)

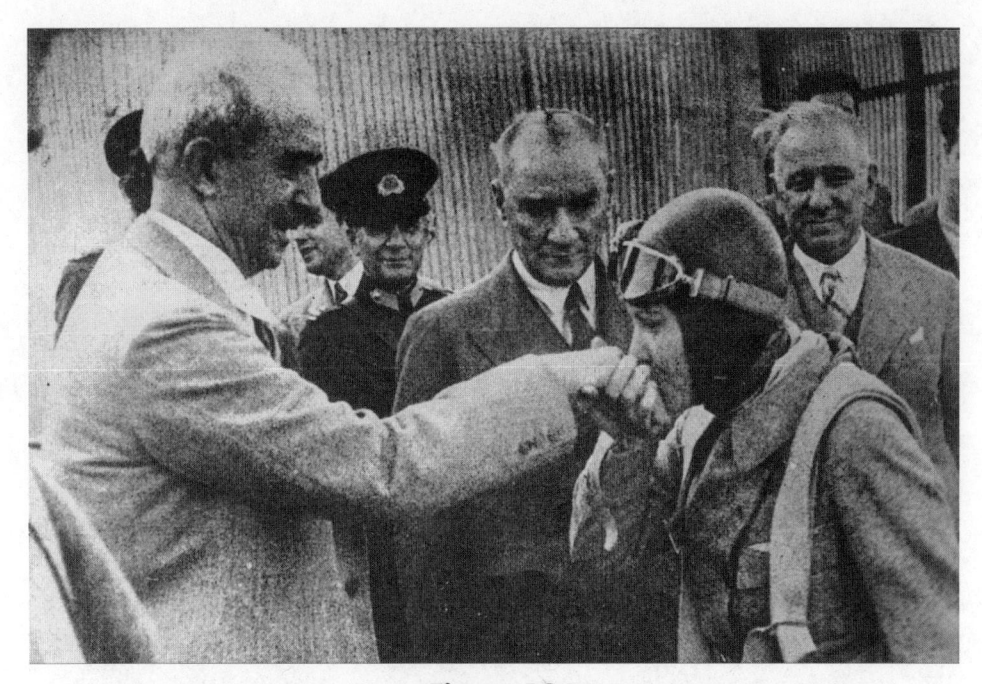

Figure 18
Sabiha Gokcen, the first Turkish women pilot, kissing the hand of Prime Minister Ismet Inönü with President Kemel Ataturk.

Article 3.6 'A brother in arms, a sister in peace ...' by Julie Wheelwright

The military has retained an ideology of masculinity more strongly than any other area of social activity (except perhaps sports). When you read the justifications given for perpetuating the exclusion of women from certain areas of activity in the armed forces, and conversely the pressures on governments to use them, keep in mind that these have direct parallels with what has happened in civilian areas of work.

> Now read Article 3.6, which you should find very straightforward. As you read make notes on the following:
> - the issue of 'front–rear' in combat, which has a parallel with 'public–private', and combat exclusion policies which restrict women to the rear (private) area of combat
> - social class in the armed forces
> - the use of arguments about physiological sex difference to justify excluding women from handling some technology
> - women's ability and enthusiasm, historically, to be involved in new developments in technology (such as flying in the early part of the twentieth century), which later become almost exclusively masculine
> - the reasons why Western governments have relaxed their sex discriminatory practices in the armed forces since the 1970s
> - what is being protected in continuing to exclude women from certain military roles.

Wheelwright argues that governments have been obliged to use women more since the abolition of the 'draft' in the USA and 'call-up' in the UK has reduced the number of suitable men coming into the forces. Alongside this are demographic changes which make fewer young men available overall. In the USA in particular these factors have also produced an increase in the proportion of recruits from the Afro-American population. Wheelwright credits the civil rights and the women's liberation movements as also having an impact. In the

USA (unlike the UK) the armed forces are not excluded from most sex discrimination legislation. Despite this, she argues, men in the military are still defending twin interests: perpetuating an ideology of masculinity and defending an almost exclusively male profession against female competition.

3.7 TECHNOLOGY AND WOMEN'S WORK IN UNDERDEVELOPED COUNTRIES

So far in this section we have looked at the participation of women in science and technology in Western Europe and the USA. However, one of the most important issues globally for feminism is understanding the impact of science and technology on women in developing countries. The final article in this section attempts to summarize the issues.

Figure 19
The traditional knitting industry, Peru

Article 3.7 'Science, technology and development' by Radha Chakravarthy

The Chakravarthy reading is very dense in terms of its style and its content – dense but not difficult. We recommend that you read it through twice. Read it through the first time to get an overall feel for the scope of the issue, then come back to each section and study it in detail.

> Now read Article 3.7, making notes on the following on your second reading.
>
> What does Chakravarthy argue about the benefits of development technology for women?
>
> What do you understand by the 'Employment, Productivity and Income Distribution paradigm' and how are women affected by it?
>
> What are the three conclusions about women's work and development that Chakravarthy draws from her reading of Palmer?
>
> Why should women be treated by development agencies as independent producers rather than members of families?

Give some examples of the effect of agricultural modernization on women.

Give some examples of industrial development and its effect on women.

How is technological obsolescence affecting women?

Finally, if you were able to create policy at the governmental level in these countries, what could you do to ensure that women achieved some benefits from the technological development process?

Chakravarthy argues that women are being affected negatively by technical changes in developing countries. Technical innovations are not usually planned with women in mind, and even when the general social impact is positive, women as a group can be affected adversely. Women's working patterns are not usually catered for, and households or families are treated as if all members were equal when in fact women's status in the household and in society is one of submission and men's dominant positions are reinforced. This means that the introduction of a technical innovation in some aspect of production, whether agricultural or industrial, has a different impact on women's employment, their productivity and consequently on their income. Women are especially badly hit by technical obsolescence. They are more likely to be employed in traditional subsistence crafts, and are likely to remain tied to the old techniques because new machinery and tools are taken over by men. Education and training are often necessary to handle the new machinery and men have better access to this. Women's work with the old methods is assigned low value and often entails health risks.

There are a number of suggestions that you could have come up with for a development policy which would benefit women. We asked Radha Chakravarthy what her recommendations would be and she gave us the following. How close are they to yours?

1. Public agencies issue a directive that there will be no further reduction in the level of employment of women. When technology is upgraded steps should be taken to retain and absorb them.

2. Applications for loans and for importing technologies should be scrutinized by the agencies concerned, with the objective of ensuring that women's labour is not displaced.

3. A list of industries which are labour-intensive in character may be prepared and a mandate issued by the policy-makers that the employment of a sizeable number of women should be provided for where technology transfer is likely to jeopardize their employment.

4. A comprehensive effort needs to be mounted and supported by fiscal, technological and administrative policies to make capital cheaper for industries which employ a large number of women.

5. Training programmes for displaced women for alternative employment should designed and made accessible.

6. There should be a regular social audit for determining the occupational health and safety of women workers and minimizing health hazards.

7. The introduction of appropriate technology should be such that women can use it to relieve their drudgery. This would call for a change in social values and norms and would help improve the status of women.

8. The trades union movement should be required to take up the cause of women and equal opportunities issues and seek to prevent sexual discrimination.

3.8 CONCLUSION

We began this section 'at the top', looking at women working in Nobel prize-winning science, and it would be fair to say that we have ended it with women close to the bottom, in terms of the value put on their work and the rewards, both financial and in status terms that they receive for it. It is important to consider in any debate about women working in science and technology why women are trapped in large numbers at the bottom as well as why they have been excluded from the top, and to note that structurally there are many similarities between the situation of women in developed and underdeveloped countries.

4
CONSUMING SCIENCE AND TECHNOLOGY (WEEKS 19–20)

4.1 TECHNOLOGY, SCIENCE AND HOUSES

This section begins 'at home' in more ways than one. You are probably reading this Study Guide in a relatively quiet area of a house or flat, probably one that you share with other people. If you are fortunate, you may have a room set aside as a study, or you may use a corner of your bedroom, or the kitchen or dining-room table when it is not being used by others. One thing that becoming an OU student will have done for you is to have made you very conscious of whether there are any parts of your home in which you can be guaranteed privacy, and which you can claim priority use. It is not unusual to hear a woman with young children complain that the only place she is ever left alone is when she locks herself in the bathroom – not an ideal place to study.

Houses are the product of social ideology and science and technology. Their design and construction reflect not only economic, environmental and technical constraints but also an ideology of family life and social organization. What does the building you live in say about the kind of lives people are expected to lead in it and the roles women in particular play there? And does it suit the lives that you and the other members of your household lead, or do you spend time thinking about knocking down internal walls, or dividing spaces in ways other than those intended by the architect/builder?

► **ACTIVITY 27** ◄

For this activity we want you to read an extract from a book entitled *Making Space: women and the man-made environment*, written by Matrix, a group of female architects and planners. We will then ask you to analyse the implicit ideology of your own home by doing a simple spatial analysis. The extract illustrates the changing ideology of family life, and especially the domestic role of women, through an analysis both of the floor plans of various English houses during the last hundred years in particular, and of the writings of some of those concerned with designing domestic dwellings. It illustrates the changing nature of women's domestic work. Please spend time studying the floor plans. You may find it useful first to read the text through, studying the plans as you go, then work through it again a second time giving your full attention to the plans. As you examine each floor plan see if you can answer the following questions:

(a) Is there an obvious sense of public and private space in the way rooms and other architectural features (e.g. back doors) are laid out?

(b) Look at the position and design of the kitchen in particular. Can you read anything from them about the ideology of women's role and the work done?

Now read the following extract.

House design and women's roles

Plans are like maps; they are a bird's-eye view of a building. They do not show what a building or a town looks like in real life. Their purpose is to describe the *relationship* between buildings, or parts of a building, in the same way as a map shows the relationship between places.

Plans show a building at a particular plane. They show a slice through the building, usually about waist height above floor level. For instance, the plan of a room in a typical nineteenth-century terrace house will look like Figure 20. Each element – door, window, staircase, wall etc. – is drawn in a particular way. Each line represents the edge of something. For example, a wall is drawn with two strong parallel lines; if there is a window in the wall there will be faint lines for the wall below the window and possibly the window sill, strong lines for the frame of the window at the sides and strong lines for the glass which the slice cuts through. All the strong lines represent elements the cut passes through; the faint lines represent the planes below it ...

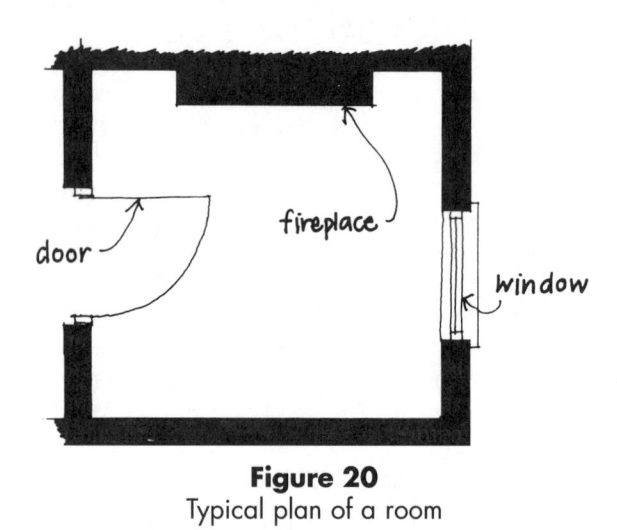

[...]

Figure 20
Typical plan of a room

Victorian gentleman's urban house, c. 1864

The plan in Figure 21 is for one of a row of London town houses ... It is taken from *The Gentleman's House* by Robert Kerr published in 1864 ... In this plan Kerr tried to translate the principles of order and status set out in his book: modest elegance, extreme propriety in personal behaviour, a sharp division between master and servant and between women and men. Kerr probably derived these ideals from an ancient Greek manual on household management for gentlemen, Xenophon's *Oeconomicus*. Xenophon was primarily a military historian. A ruthless concern for efficiency, more suited to the management of an army than a household, pervades both works.

[...]

In his book Kerr attempts to set up a complicated hierarchy of age, sex, class and household activities by their placing within the plan. As a rule of thumb status decreases from front to back and by increasing distances away from the two main floors (ground and first). Segregation is maintained between servants and family by separate staircases.

Kerr was very concerned with privacy, which he considered the primary concern of the house ... At this time and with this class, children are still placed about parallel with servants.

[...]

Finally Kerr emphasized the importance of planning the working areas on a different basis to the rest of the house (which was to focus on comfort). In contrast the kitchens and other servant spaces were to be based on efficiency and function. (See Figure 22.)

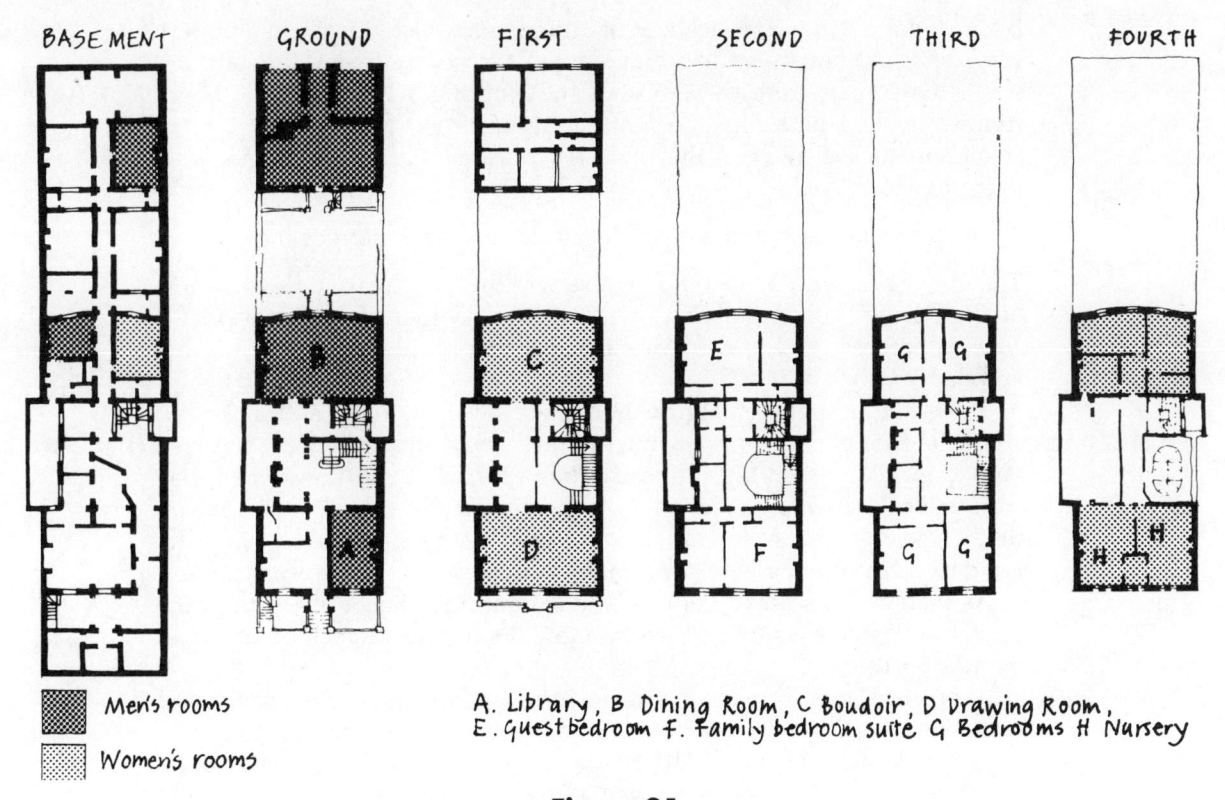

Figure 21
'A Gentleman's Town House', designed by Robert Kerr in 1864.
This redrawn plan shows the separation of men's and women's realms

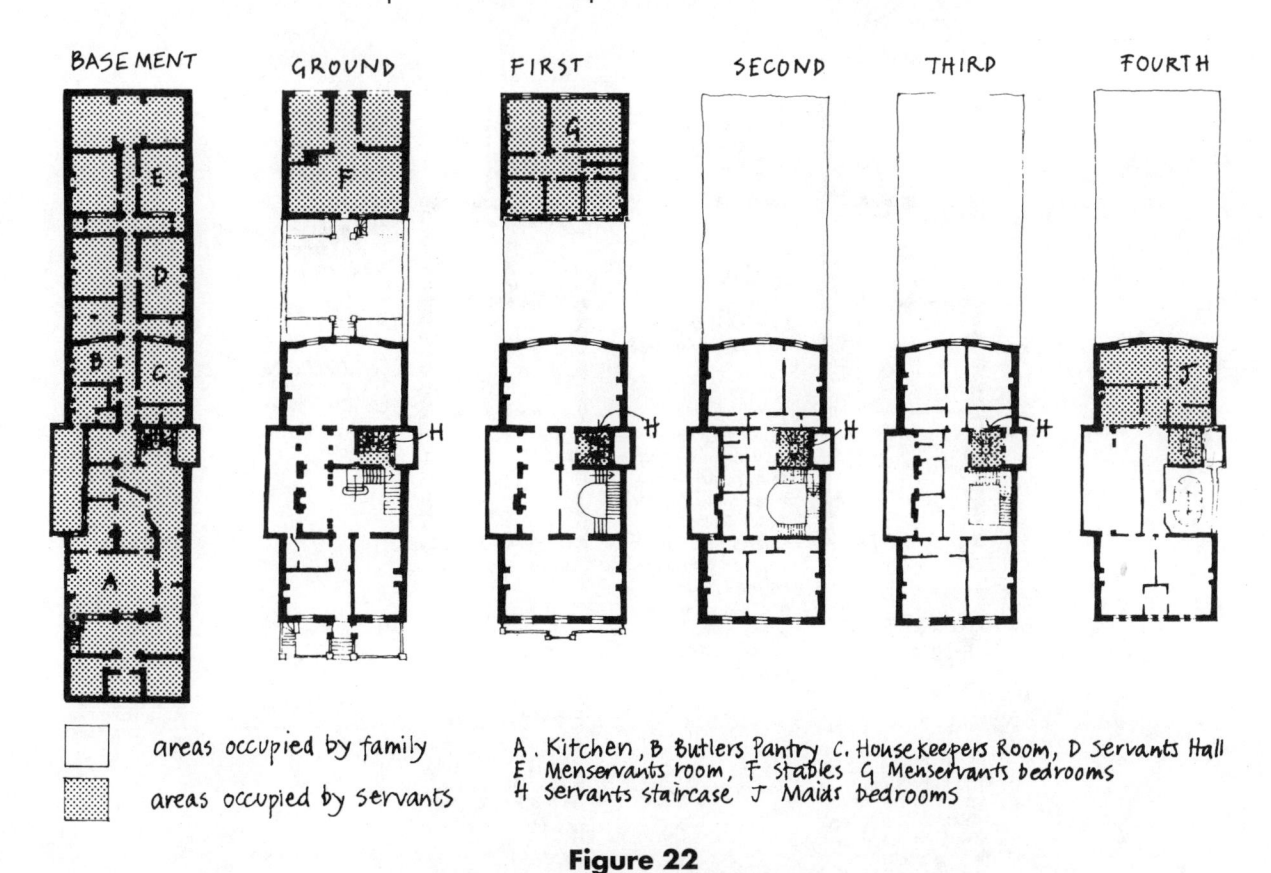

Men's rooms
Women's rooms

A. Library, B Dining Room, C Boudoir, D Drawing Room,
E. Guest bedroom F. Family bedroom suite G Bedrooms H Nursery

Figure 22
'A Gentlemen's Town House', 1864.
This redrawn plan shows the segregation of the servants from the family

areas occupied by family
areas occupied by servants

A. Kitchen, B Butlers Pantry C. Housekeepers Room, D Servants Hall
E Menservants room, F Stables G Menservants bedrooms
H Servants staircase J Maids bedrooms

Even today there are echoes of these Victorian ideas in modern semi-detached houses with ground floors focused on entertainment and status. Of course, from the 1930s all the working activities of the house from pantry to laundry had been fitted into one room – the kitchen – often small and tucked away at the back. At the same time the servants were being replaced by the wife ...

Late nineteenth and early twentieth-century urban terrace

The most basic form of 'through' house was the 'two up, two down'. Most of these have been demolished as there was no room for improvements such as bathrooms, and the stairs in particular were often steep, narrow and dangerous.

The example shown in Figure 23 is more substantial and still makes up a large part of our present housing in inner urban areas, often modernized with grants. Although they appear to be in the inner city now, when they were built they were on the edge of the city, in the suburbs. This meant that it was only better-off workers who could afford them, those who were not dependent upon a wife's earnings to supplement the family income.

As soon as houses had both back and front, the kitchen was put at the back, just as in the elaborate Victorian town house the kitchen occupied an interior position ...

A scullery was provided for washing clothes, pots and pans, and facilities like a ventilated larder and running water made domestic work much easier. Cooking and eating meals took place in the back room, along with most other everyday activities. The Women's Housing

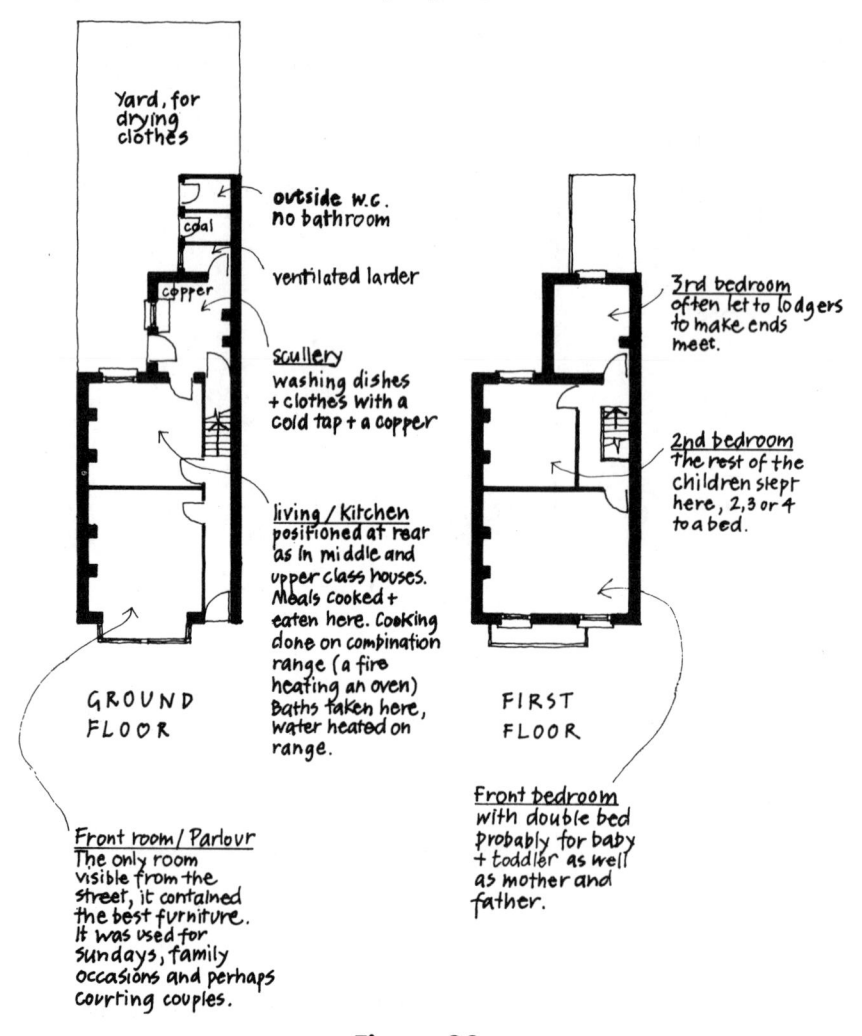

Figure 23
A typical terraced house, built extensively by speculative firms from the end of the nineteenth century

Sub-Committee report of 1918 which surveyed the opinions of working-class women ... showed that they would have preferred a separate workplace as well as this back room. However, these women also wanted to retain the parlour or front room ...

Plans like this make a clear distinction between back and front: friends come to the back door via an alley, acquaintances are received at the front and are met in the parlour where the best possessions are kept.

[...]

Thirties semi-detached suburban house

Variants of the plan shown in Figure 24 were built in virtually every town in the country, in the sudden expansion of home ownership to the middle class and a few of the better-paid members of the working class. The typical thirties plan represents the ultimate paring down of the status-conscious large Victorian town house.

[...]

Houses built for sale retained a kitchen so that cooking and eating could be separated with the possibility of employing domestic help in the kitchen ...

The builders of semi-detached houses used modern bathrooms and kitchens as the selling point for their houses. Advertisements for the period show photographs of housewives who appear delighted with their

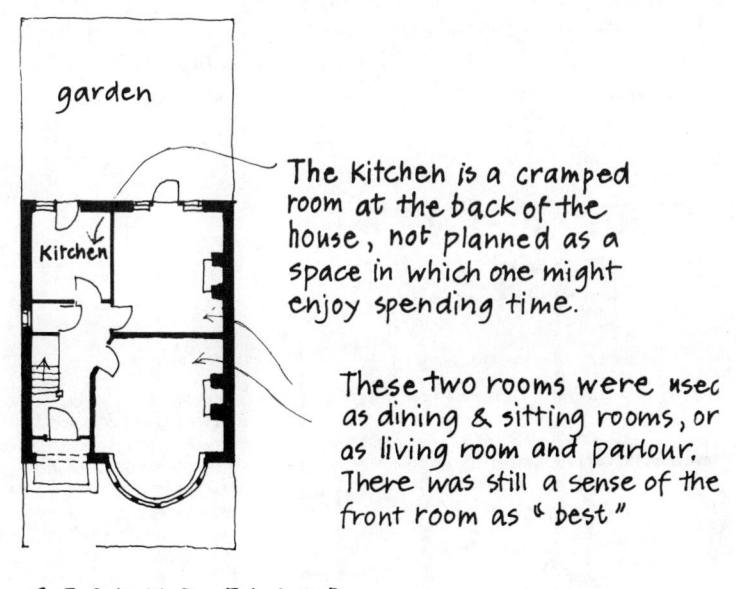

The kitchen is a cramped room at the back of the house, not planned as a space in which one might enjoy spending time.

These two rooms were used as dining & sitting rooms, or as living room and parlour. There was still a sense of the front room as "best"

GROUND FLOOR

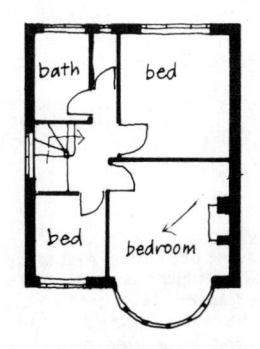

Like the front room downstairs the 'master bedroom' was also furnished to impress, with dressing table & 3 panelled mirror in the bay window

FIRST FLOOR

Figure 24
A semi-detached suburban house built in the 1930s. Aimed at the rising class of owner-occupiers, this design retained elements of the status-conscious Victorian town house

new chromium-plated bathrooms. Of course, for many this was probably the first time they had had a fitted bath, or many of the other improvements in heating, plumbing and cooking facilities. In this period consumer durables such as electric irons and vacuum cleaners became available for a mass market. Builders often gave these away too, as an inducement to buy. Middle-class women became associated with the consumption of goods within the house.

Later developments towards more open-plan houses, whilst perhaps using available space more effectively and breaking down traditional divisions between formality and informality in behaviour, nonetheless often also meant that women had to keep much more of the ground floor tidy, clean and ready for 'show' and that many more consumer durables might become part of the display of 'best' possessions for status and dignity.

Post-war council house

Council house building in the immediate post-war years was given high priority. The houses were much more spacious than any council housing built before or since, and council houses were intended to appeal to all sections of society, living side by side in 'mixed communities'. At the same time, these houses strongly reflect the post-war idealization of family life, seeing the house as a cheerful and comfortable place where wives would find homemaking a pleasure and not a burden.

[...]

The plan shown in Figure 25 continues the single front-to-back living-room from the 1920s, but by now cooking has been removed to the kitchen, so this room is purely for family relaxation and leisure.

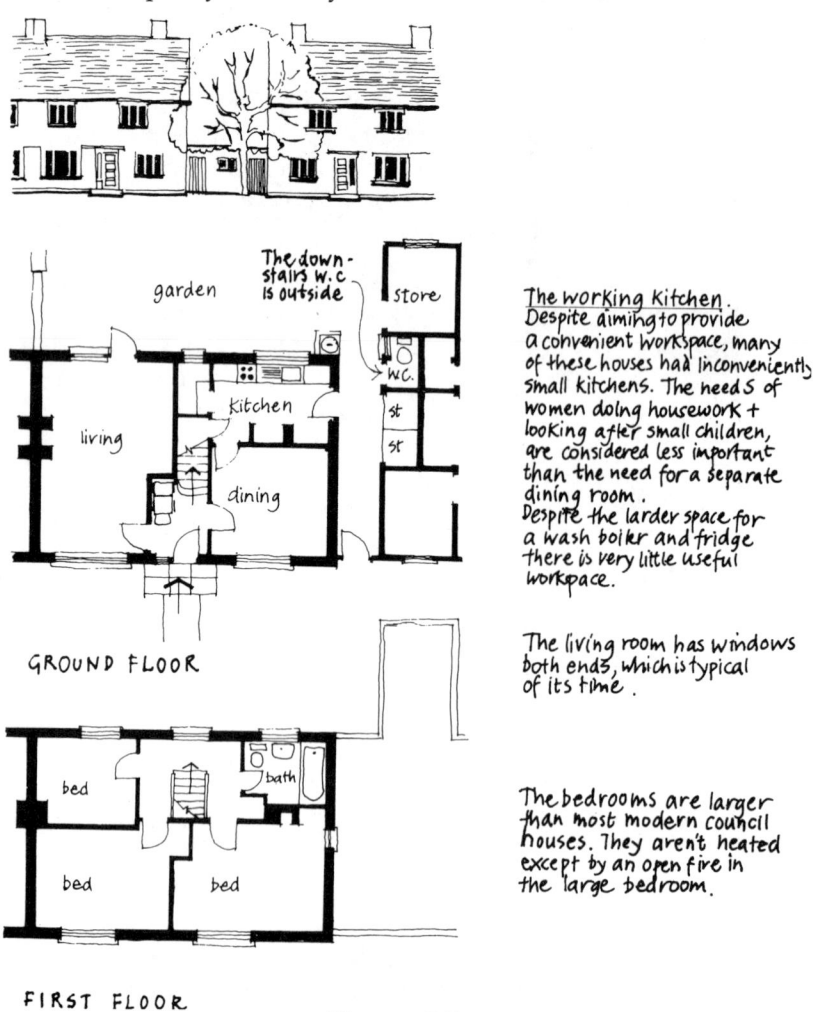

Figure 25
This council house, designed in 1949, reflects the post-war idealization of family life

Finally, the kitchen remained small, in some local authority areas, despite continuing demands through this period for families to eat here. The Parker-Morris Report ... admitted to this demand and commented on earlier plans which saw eating in the kitchen as a working-class habit, and deliberately tried to prevent it by not allowing enough space ...

The sixties and the seventies

The amount of space provided in housing declined steadily throughout the 1950s ... In order to allow individuals to follow more fully their own lives within the family house structure, the Parker-Morris report [of 1961] recommended more space and better heating in the bedrooms. This would allow all rooms to be used during the day; children could use their bedrooms as 'own rooms' for study, play or entertaining friends. At the same time, Government design guides such as *Housing the Family* ..., which architects used for guidelines in designing actual houses, perpetuated a very traditional picture of the nuclear family and women's role within it.

The house plan from *Housing the Family* shown in Figure 26 reflects some of these ambiguities in attempting to describe and fulfil the needs of many different individuals within a small, narrow frontage, family house. It provides, for instance, a small 'spare' room at the front of the house to be used as an extra bedroom, sewing room and so on. Of course this room also serves (rather like the library in the Kerr plan) to hide the more 'private' family areas behind.

[...]

GROUND FLOOR

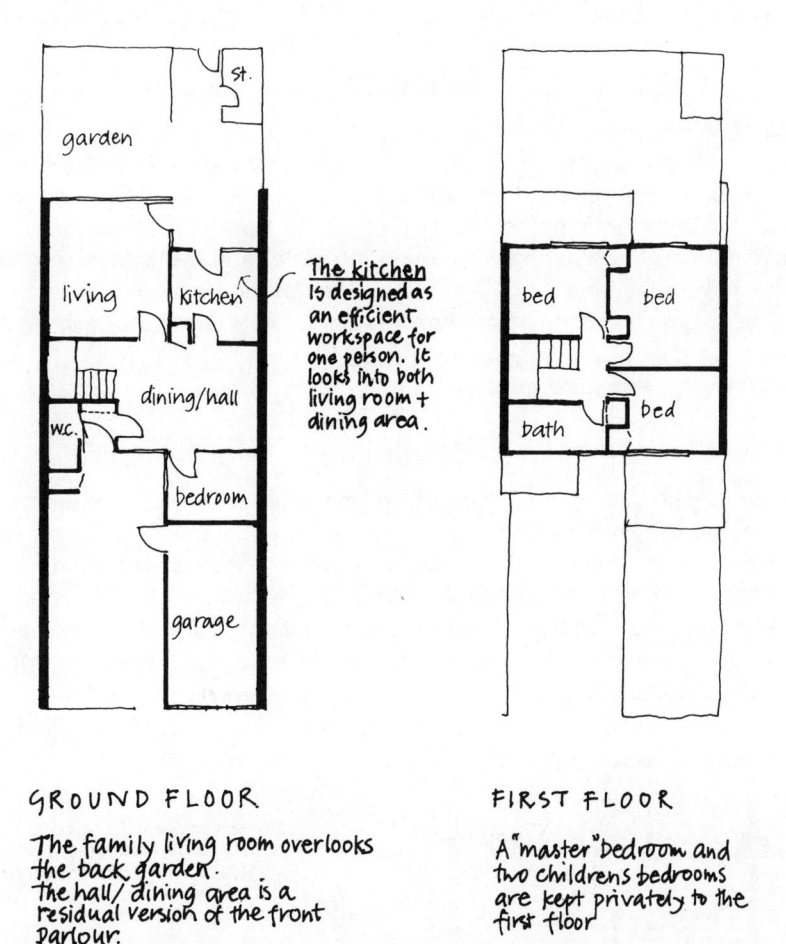

The family living room overlooks the back garden.
The hall/dining area is a residual version of the front parlour.

FIRST FLOOR

A "master" bedroom and two childrens bedrooms are kept privately to the first floor.

The kitchen is designed as an efficient workspace for one person. It looks into both living room + dining area.

Figure 26
This 1960s' design for a five-person nuclear family is still in current use

The kitchen acts as a hub to the plan, looking into both the living-room and dining area. It is therefore neither a separate workplace (to contain noise and smells) nor physically part of the other rooms in the house. It is still planned on the workbench principle ... and designed around one person, almost certainly presumed to be the wife ...

Now refer back to Activity 27 before reading the comments below.

COMMENT

All the houses' 'private' areas are at the back. These are the areas where women work, such as the scullery (the kitchen), suggesting that only those with access to the private space of the family use this door. There are problems such as siting a toilet downstairs at the back of the house (until the 1960s), making it necessary for a visitor to pass through the kitchen to use it. The development of separate bedrooms also illustrates a felt need for privacy between family members at least while they are sleeping. Only in the 1960s' house is there an extra room on the 'public' ground floor which can be multi-functional.

The major features of the kitchen seem to be that it is low status, and it should remain invisible. It is always at the back of the house and, as Matrix remarks, it is squeezed into the smallest possible space to leave more space for other public activities. It is also kept as a separate room, so that those in the dining area do not see the work of cooking or washing. It is interesting that in the nineteenth-century terraced house there was a combined living-room/kitchen; washing was relegated to the rear of the house.

► ACTIVITY 28 ◄

Many of us live in the kinds of houses described by Matrix, although structural alterations may have been made over the years to cope with different family preferences. Use the grid on the next page to draw a floor plan of your home. Although you do not need to produce an accurate scaled drawing, you will appreciate from the Matrix sketches that having the plan roughly to scale is important. If you did this activity in detail you could spend many hours on it. We suggest that you spend no more than two hours.

COMMENT

Look at the space designed for the person doing the domestic work in your home. How big is it? Is it situated in a public area of the house? Does it have a pleasant view from its windows? Look at the way your home is occupied. Do some individuals occupy more spaces than others? Do you have a garden, and if so who works in it and who occupies it? Are there outbuildings, for example a shed, and if so who has 'ownership' of the space in that? In fact, is the space in your house gendered?

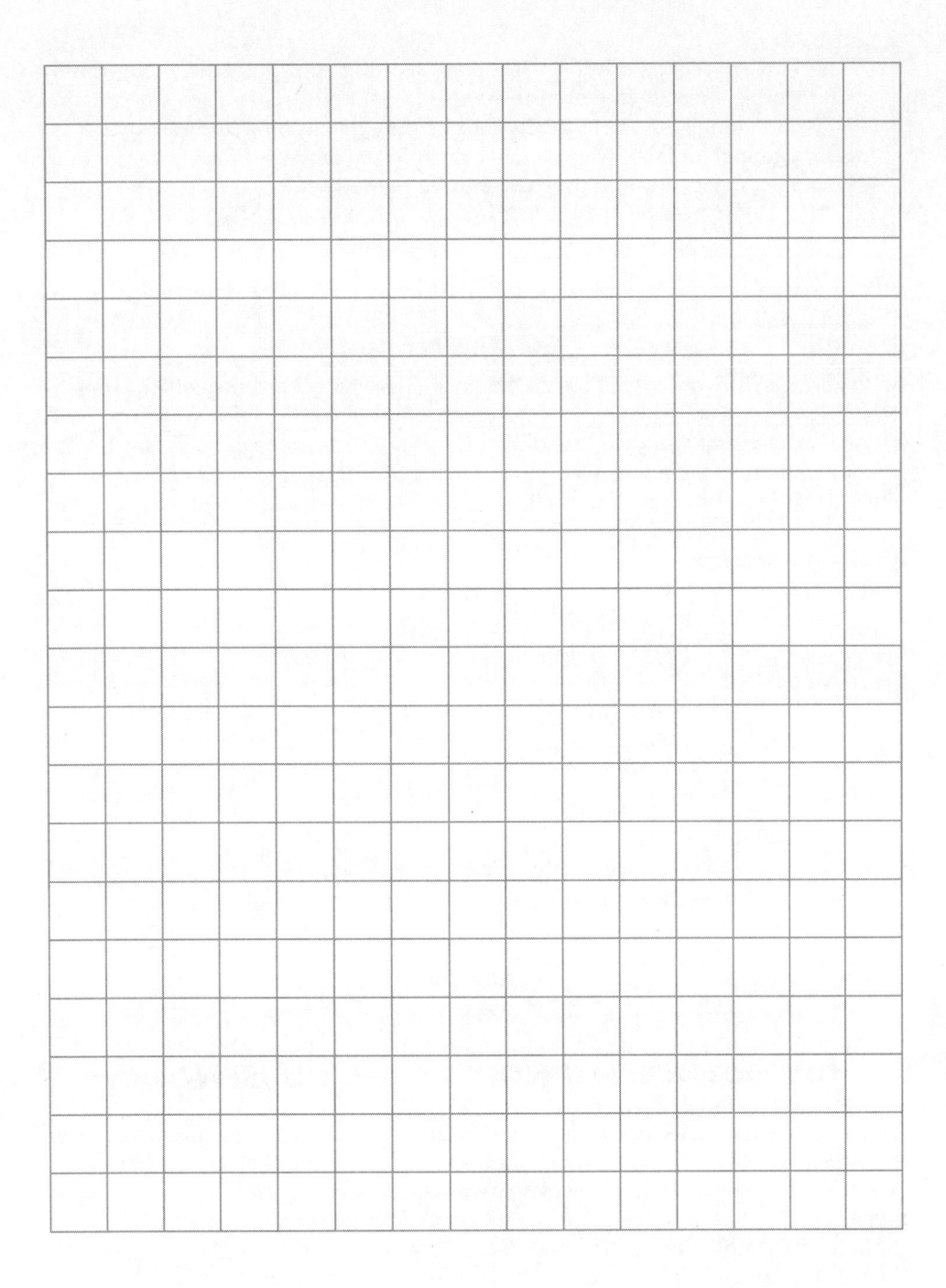

The example below is those of one of the authors. Since the house is of an unusual design a section and elevation have also been included. Compare your plan to ours. In our house the kitchen window commands a view of the street and public rooms are at the rear and overlook the garden. The kitchen/dining areas are separated and the kitchen is too small for a family to eat in. Now you have a sketch of your own home you might like to think about how the space could be organized differently to break down the sexual division of labour, and to make domestic work both more visible and more pleasant.

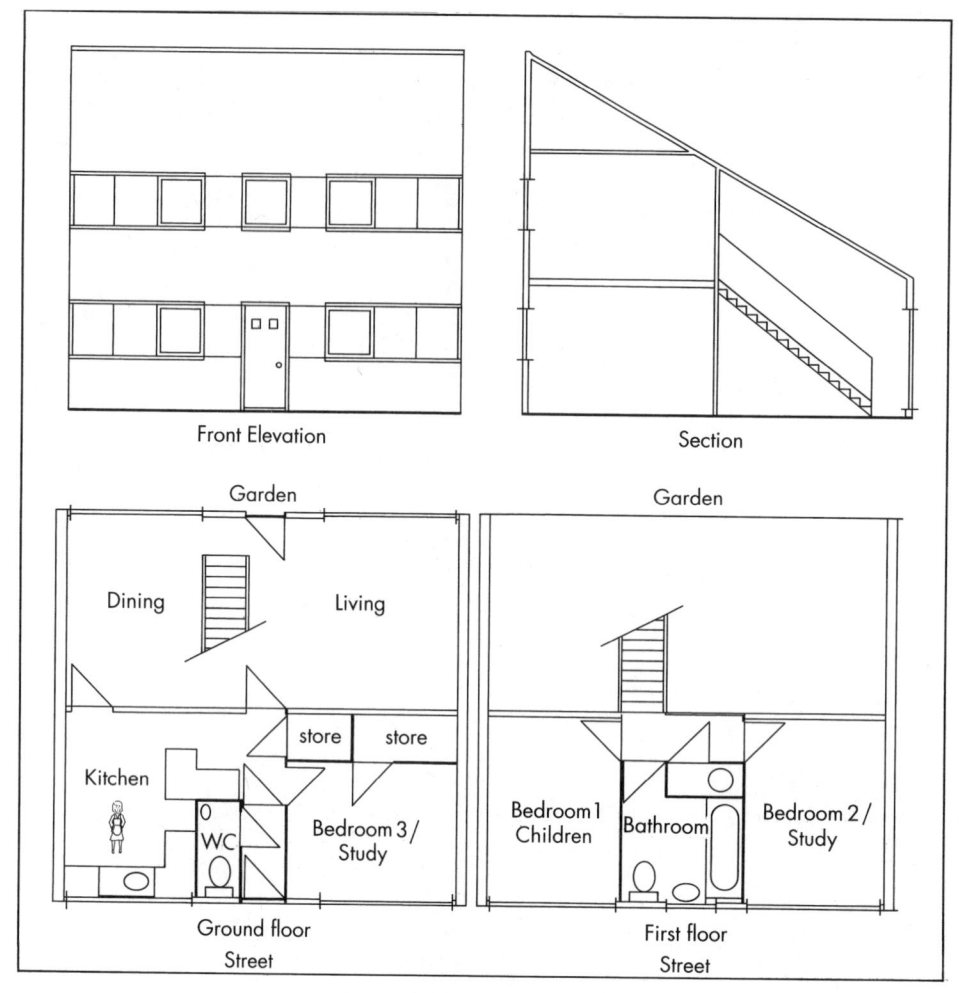

Figure 27
House plan

4.2 SCIENCE, TECHNOLOGY AND HOUSEWORK

Unless you have some particular interest in architecture or planning, you are not likely to have thought much about the buildings that constitute your environment as technology. However, by now this course should be making you more critical of the architecture of both public and private space, and more aware of the ideologies of class and gender that are implicit in this architecture. Both public and private buildings are places of activity for women, although architects and planners have been criticized for producing public architecture which ignores the needs of women with young children, and domestic architecture which presumes each house contains a 'privatized' housewife. The Matrix extract and activity you have just done have demonstrated how domestic ideology is embedded in the bricks and mortar (or timber and cladding!) of private homes. Chapter 4 of *Defining Women* discussed feminist analysis of the ideology of housework. Here we will examine how this ideology is embedded in the technology for housework.

In Book Three the two articles which deal with domestic technology have been placed in the chapter called 'Consuming Science and Technology'. In traditional economic analysis housework was consumption rather than production because no saleable commodities were produced – and if they were it was redefined as 'cottage industry' – and housework was unwaged – when it was waged it was redefined as service work and the houseworker reclassified 'domestic servant'. Even so, the labour involved in housework was recognized: Figure 28 shows a 1930s' Coca Cola advertisement where Coca Cola is offered as a *scientific* remedy to the exhaustion of housework.

You WALK 8 miles a day just in Housework

Up and down. In and out. Round and round. Eight miles a day just in housework. Of course, you get tired. Pause! Use your head to save your heels. Refresh yourself with an ice-cold bottle of Coca-Cola from your refrigerator, and rebound to normal. ● An ice-cold Coca-Cola is more than just a drink. It's a very particular kind of drink—combining those pleasant, wholesome substances which foremost scientists say do most in restoring you to your normal self. Really delicious, it invites a pause—*the pause that refreshes.*

Pause . . refresh yourself
Bounce back to normal

Figure 28
Advertisement for Coca Cola, 1930s

Feminist analysis has argued that housework is production and can be analysed as such if economic and sociological models are revised to make women's work visible. When defined as economically productive work it becomes possible to ask whether or not technical change has increased the productivity of housewives as it has of other workers.

Turn now to the Introduction to Chapter 4 and read to the end of the paragraph beginning 'The poem "Dry" by Jean Binta Breeze ...' (pp. 232–5).

This introduces the articles by Wajcman and Agarwal which discuss aspects of domestic technology from different world views.

Article 4.1 'Domestic technology: labour-saving or enslaving?' by Judy Wajcman

Now read Article 4.1. Allow yourself up to two hours on this article. Read it through once for the general argument and then a second time, to make notes on the ideas of the different theorists discussed by Wajcman:

- Talcott Parsons
- Ruth Schwartz Cowan
- Cynthia Cockburn
- David Morley
- Jonathan Gershuny
- Claude Fischer.

Frances Gabe is an inventor rather than a theorist. She built her self-cleaning house rather than wrote about it.

Wajcman also mentions Charlotte Perkins Gilman, Engels, Bebel and Kollontai. The following brief biographies might help you:

Charlotte Perkins Gilman ((1860–1935) American feminist and writer. She wrote widely on women's issues at the turn of the century, and her most enjoyable work is arguably *Herland*, her feminist fictional Utopia.

Ferdinand August Bebel (1840-1913), leader of the German Social Democrat movement, wrote widely on socialism including the status of women.

Alexandra Kollontai (1872-1952), Russian feminist and revolutionary. She wrote both fiction and socialist analysis.

Also make notes on the following.

Identify the main aim of the author in writing the article.

Would you classify her position as technological determinist or social determinist?

What are the main points of the feminist analysis of developments in domestic technology? How does Wajcman differ from Cowan in her analysis?

Note the contribution of domestic technology to the development of 'private' or individualized domestic labour and relate this to the development of domestic houses illustrated in the Matrix article.

Give examples from the article and your own experience of shifts in the family from production to consumption of goods or services and vice versa.

Wajcman gives her aim at the end of the second paragraph: 'to explore the way the design and promotion of domestic technologies have been shaped by existing ideologies of gender'.

This alone should suggest that Wajcman's position is closer to that of social determinism. You may have also picked further examples from her piece. Wajcman is very critical of what she calls the 'technicist orientation' of Gershuny's work. Make sure that you can represent both Gershuny's position and the argument Wajcman makes against it.

Just ask these lovely Brides

if they intend to be old SCRUBWOMEN at Forty

It sounds ridiculous, doesn't it? Girls so fresh and lovely, with soft hands and all the eagerness of youth.

We think of these girls of 1931 as strictly moderns. But are they really as modern as they look? Do they keep house in the modern fashion? Or are there still *floor-scrubbers* among them? Will any of their friends ever catch them down on all fours, at the ugly, back-breaking, hand roughening job of scrubbing floors, linoleum and woodwork?

These girls don't *have* to become old scrubwomen at 40. Modern science has done much to take the drudgery out of their housework. There is Johnson's Wax, for example—and the improved Johnson Electric Floor Polisher. With these two household aids every home can have beautiful floors, protected against scuffing and scratching, without any more scrubbing and with very little effort of maintenance.

The wax is easily applied with a long-handled lamb's wool applier. The floors are quickly polished just to the right degree with the Johnson Electric Polisher, that glides swiftly and without effort over varnished or unvarnished wood and linoleum surfaces. Thereafter, dust is removed in an instant with a dry mop. That's the Johnson's Wax story. Dirt cannot penetrate the hard, waxed surface. Worn spots are quickly renewed by touching up with a little wax on a cloth. And as for scrubbing—it's a thing of the past.

For furniture, woodwork, leather and automobiles, too—Johnson's Wax is the great protector, beautifier and labor-saver. It makes a hard, beautiful surface, safe against scratches, finger-marks, water-spots, stains.

In both liquid and paste form, it is on sale at hardware, grocery, paint, drug and department stores. In every community dealers **RENT** out the Johnson Electric Polisher at $2.00 a day.

If you have any floor, furniture or woodwork problems, write to S. C. Johnson & Son at Racine—for 45 years authorities on the care and maintenance of these surfaces.

Shi-nup FOR SILVER
At last you can get this remarkable polish—at your own store—for silver, glassware, enamel and nickel. Now made by S. C. Johnson & Son.

• Complete Floor Maintenance outfit includes new Johnson Electric Floor Polisher, Johnson's Wax (paste and liquid), lamb's wool applier and Johnson gold-striped floor duster.

• S. C. Johnson & Son, Dept. SP 12, Racine, Wisconsin. Please send me a 25c bottle of Johnson's Wax Polish to try. I am enclosing 10c for postage.

NAME
ADDRESS
CITY   STATE

Figure 29
Advertisement for Johnson's Wax, United States, 1931

The feminist argument makes the following points:
- unpaid domestic production is work
- domestic work is gendered, reflecting gendered ideology about women's and men's roles

- the use of technology in the home is also gendered, reinforced by the gendered nature of technical skills for waged work (remember Cockburn in Article 3.4)
- the proportion of time women spend on domestic work is not decreased by technological developments, although it changes
- technical change is driven by the economics of business and moulded by social ideology.

Cowan believes that women make choices from amongst the technologies available, and their choices are based on moral values and basic desires, mainly those for 'autonomy' and 'privacy'. Wajcman gives much more emphasis to the 'structural' nature of social forces, arguing that in reality women had little choice since there were no real alternatives to the privatized family, with its privatized domestic work.

Wajcman quotes the production of food and clothing and the provision of health care as cases where the household has moved from production to consumption. If our grandparents are to be believed, 'entertainment' also fitted this model. The family has become a producer rather than a consumer of transport – for people and goods. Home decorating and 'do-it-yourself' home renovation have also become areas of production whereas in the early years of the century 'painter and decorator' and even 'paperhanger' were skilled working-class jobs bought in by a family. Laundry is another aspect of domestic work which many families, not only the middle-class, once 'sent out' and are now likely to do with a 'privatized' automatic machine. I hope you have thought of others.

There are ways in which we can begin to examine our own domestic environments and assess both the usefulness of the technology we own and the division of labour over household tasks, even perhaps the necessity of doing some of it at all.

▶ ACTIVITY 29 ◀

One of the simplest things to do is to make a list of all the equipment and gadgets that you use to do housework. Remember those invisible ones like the hot-water tank, and the services like refuse collection. Then for each ask the following questions:

(a) Who benefits from it?

(b) Who operates it?

(c) How often is it used?

(d) Who cleans and looks after it?

(e) How often is it cleaned/maintained?

(f) Who repairs it when it goes wrong?

(g) What would be the effect on you if you did not have it?

(h) What would be the effect on the other members of the household if you did not have it?

COMMENT

As an example this is my personal response to **the cooker**. I wonder how close it is to yours? If cooking is your hobby it will look very different.

(a) We all apparently benefit.

(b) Me mostly – sometimes partner.

(c) Daily.

(d) Me mostly, sometimes partner.

(e) Cleaned a couple of times a week (max.).

(f) Service engineer.

(g) I'd have a lot less work to do. Most of what *I* eat isn't cooked, mostly I cook to produce meals for the majority.

(h) They would have to change their eating habits dramatically and they wouldn't like it.

But if I take **the iron** – a tool used almost exclusively by me, my responses to (g) and (h) above would be very different from that of the cooker.

(g) It would have a dramatic effect on me – I'd hate wearing un-ironed clothes.

(h) No one else would care, they wear ironed clothes now because I care and iron them!

In this case the usefulness of a piece of technology and the work associated with it are due almost solely to an ideology of visual appearance rather than utility. A shirt is no more useful ironed than crumpled.

Both the Matrix and the Wajcman articles have used historical examples for comparison, to show change over time. The changes they have described can be identified in the lives of individuals and their families. For example, what changes have occurred in three generations of your own family, or someone close to you?

ACTIVITY 30

Fill the blank table given overleaf. Choose three generations of women *at a similar period in their life cycles* – the example given (from one of us) is that of three women with pre-school children.

Note whether the women you choose were urban or rural, and in which country they lived, their social class and the number of children they had. Underneath list the household technology used to carry out regular domestic tasks and any services used. If you choose your mother you may remember details or can ask. In other cases you may have to interview and investigate.

Grandmother (1920s)	Mother (1950s)	Myself (1980s)
Urban UK occupation – M.C. – small shopkeeper p/t Children – 3	Urban UK occupation – W.C. p/t nurse Children – 2	Urban UK occupation – M.C. full/time academic Children – 2

coal fires
coal-fired range for cooking & water
outside toilet flush
bathroom with plumbed water, and gas geyser
electricity – for lights only
	coal fires
	coal-fired hot-water tank
	flush-toilet (inside)
	gas boiler for washing
	+ wringer & posser
	gas cooker
	
	vacuum cleaner
	cooking gadgets (mechanical)
	   whisk
	   mincer
	   scales etc.
	fitted bathroom
	electricity
		central heating (thermostat-controlled)
		hot water
		flush toilets (2)
		plumbed automatic washer
		electricity
		gas cooker – with timer
		automatic ignition
		vacuum cleaner
		telephone
		
		drying cupboard
		cooking gadgets various
		   liquidiser
		   electric kettle
		   coffee maker (electrical)
		fridge
		freezer
		car

services used
  a grandmother for childcare
  a cook (paid)
  a general domestic for all cleaning (paid)
  groceries delivered
	services used
	  door to door deliveries – milk, butcher, ice cream
	  occasional childcare from grandmother, and neighbour
		services used
		  1 morning per week cleaner (paid)
		  nursery for children (paid)

Grandmother's generation	**Mother's generation**	**Myself or my generation**
Household technology available:	*Household technology available:*	*Household technology available:*
Services used:	*Services used:*	*Services used:*

COMMENT

It is most interesting if, afterwards, you can compare your table with others, done by other students or by you using other women. In this way you could explore the difference in lifestyles among women who, although of the same generation, were of different, national, regional or class backgrounds. For example, the technology available to rural British women of the 1920s and '30s, in particular no gas or electricity, was enormously different from that of urban women where electrification and the provision of 'town' gas were established.

Look at how many differences were due to class, historical period or area of the country, perhaps even different country. Ask yourself how many developments have occurred in the direction you would have chosen, how many developments are perhaps retrograde. I think you might be surprised to find that you envy some of the housework arrangements that your grandmother had. However, I don't intend to romanticize the past; replacing your domestic technology by other women working for you is a solution with its own problems.

4.3 DOMESTIC TECHNOLOGY IN ECOLOGICAL AND ECONOMIC CRISIS

The reading by Chakravarthy in Chapter 3 introduced the issues of gender, technology and development. Consequently her discussion is wide-ranging, encompassing a variety of significant political and technical issues that confront anyone concerned to optimize the benefits of development for Third World women. The piece you will now study by Bina Agarwal concentrates on one important ecological and technological problem for developing countries – the scarcity of fuel for domestic purposes. She describes a particular kind of low technology solution – the design and construction by rural women of woodburning stoves.

Article 4.2 'Cold hearths and barren slopes: the woodfuel crisis in the Third World' by Bina Agarwal

Article 4.2 is condensed from a much longer book in which Agarwal also discusses tree-planting schemes, and ways of converting wood into other, more efficient fuels such as charcoal. She looks at the social as well as the technical consequences of the woodfuel crisis and potential solutions. The piece you will read concentrates on the impact of this ecological crisis on the domestic work and lives of women, and demonstrates optimistically how in the most 'low tech' environments women can contribute to the design and construction of technical innovations.

> Read the first three sections of Article 4.2, stopping at the end of the section 'Implications of shortages' (pp. 255–8). Make notes on the following:
> - The importance of wood for fuel in developing countries, i.e. what percentage of all domestic fuel does it provide?
> - The important effects deforestation has had on the lives of women in particular.

Agarwal gives estimates of 75–89 per cent of all fuelwood being used for domestic purposes, and very little used in industry. But this has to be understood in relation to the figures she quotes about the proportion provided by fuelwood of total energy used by a country. If woodfuel provides one-third of all energy in India, and most of this is used for domestic purposes, then we can presume that the other two-thirds (fuel from elsewhere) is used by industry. But if wood and charcoal provide 90 per cent of all fuel in parts of Africa and most of this is used for domestic purposes, this reflects the non-industrialized nature of the country. You may be interested that in the UK wood provides less than 1 per cent of all fuel; its use is restricted to wood-fired boilers and open fires usually in rural areas. However, in Norway, Sweden and Finland, timber is the second major source of fuel energy after hydroelectricity.

The important effects on women's lives of deforestation are:

1. More work for women collecting woodfuel
   (a) more time spent
   (b) more effort expended

   therefore less available time and energy for other activities such as agriculture.

2. More time spent on cooking, more problems with cooking (e.g. boiling water).

3. Deteriorating nutritional standards, probably also due to other effects of ecological crisis – desertification often follows deforestation.

4. Lowering of water table – means more work for women – with concomitant effects on heath.

5. Loss of schooling for girl children.

► **ACTIVITY 31** ◄

Table 7 gives in tabular form more extensive information on the time taken to collect domestic firewood. The table illustrates both the problem of collecting woodfuel and the problem of assembling such a table using data from a variety of sources.

Read the table carefully and then answer the following questions:

(a) In which countries is the crisis worst with respect to time spent gathering fuel and distance travelled to gather it? Is there a relationship between distance travelled and time spent?

(b) What problems are involved in using the table to build a coherent picture?

Table 7 Time taken and distance travelled for firewood collection, by region

Country	Region	Year of data	Firewood collection[1] Time taken	Distance travelled	Data source[3]
Asia					
Nepal	Tinan (hills)	1978	3 hr/day	n.a.	Stone (1982)
	Pangua (hills)	late 1970s	4-5 hr/bundle	n.a.	Bajracharya (1983a)
	n.a.	n.a.	0.62 hr/day	n.a.	Acharya and Bennett (1981)
India	Chamoli (hills)				
	(a) Dwing	1982	5 hr/day[2]	over 5 km	Swaminathan (1984)
	(b) Pakhi		4 hr/day	over 3 km	
	Gujarat (plains)	1980	once every 4 days	n.a.	Nagbrahman and Sambrani (1983)
	(a) forested		once every 2 days	4-5 km	
	(b) depleted				
	(c) severely depleted		4-5 hr/day	5 km	
	Madhya Pradesh (plains)	1980	1-2 times/week	5-7 km	Chand and Bezboruah (1980)
	Kumaon Hills	1982	3 days/week	5.4 km/trip	Folger and Dewan (1983)
	Karnataka (plains)	n.a.	1 hr/day	10 km	Batliwala (1983)
	Garhwal (hills)	n.a.	5 hr/day	n.a.	Agarwal (1983)
Bangladesh	Chargopal	1977	0.4 hr/day	n.a.	Cain *et al.* (1979)
Indonesia	Java	1972-73	0.3 hr/day	n.a.	White (1976)
Africa					
Sahel	n.a.	c. 1977	3 hr/day	10 km	Floor (1977)
Niger	n.a.	1981	3-4 hr/day	n.a.	Ki-Zerbo (1981)
Burkina Faso	n.a.	c. 1977	4 hr/day	n.a.	Ernst (1977)
(Upper Volta)	n.a.	n.a.	4.5 hr/day	n.a.	Ernst (1977)
Sudan	Bara	1966-67	0.33 hr/day	n.a.	Digerness (1977)
		1976-77	1-2 hr/day	n.a.	
Tanzania	(hills)	1975-76	1.6 hr/day	n.a.	Fleuret and Fleuret (1978)
Kenya	n.a.	n.a.	3-3.5 hr/day	n.a.	Earthscan (1978)
Ghana	n.a.	n.a.	4-5 trips/week	2.5-7 miles	DEVRES (1980)
Latin America					
Peru	(a) Pincos (highlands)	1981	1.33 hr/day	n.a.	Skar (1982)
	(b) Matapuan (highlands)	1981	1.67 hr/day	n.a.	

Notes:
[1] Firewood is noted to be collected principally by women and children in all the studies listed, with the exception of Java where the labour put in is primarily by men.
[2] Average, computed from information given in the study.
[3] Full sources not given, but included here to show diversity of source material.
n.a. = Information not available.
Source: Agarwal, 1986, pp. 18–19

COMMENT

(a) The table indicates that the crisis is severe in most areas of India for which there is data and in the Sahel, Niger, Burkina Faso, Ghana and Kenya in Africa. The relationship between time spent and distance is not straightforward: for example, in the Floor study in the Sahel women spent 3 hrs a day travelling 10 km to gather wood, whereas in Garhwal India women spent 5 hrs a day to cover the same distance. This suggests that the density of fuel in an area is important in determining how long is spent, but since we don't know whether the needs of a family are the same in Sahel and Garhwal we don't know how much women are collecting.

(b) This brings us on to problems with a table like this which include some of the following:

- The studies were done at different times – earliest 1966-67, latest 1982. We can safely presume there have been ecological and economic changes in these countries in twenty years.
- Many studies do not provide information on aspects of the table – in particular, distance travelled (hard data to collect).
- Some times are reported as hours per day, others as days per week. There is no way to compare these accurately.

These criticisms do not make the table, or Agarwal's discussion of the data in the text, invalid. But they do show the problems a researcher has when trying to summarize information and make comparisons when that information has come from a variety of sources and other researchers.

Now complete your reading of Article 4.2 (pp. 258–65), making notes on the following.

What are the potential technical solutions to the woodfuel crisis?

Distinguish between innovation and diffusion.

What are the general factors involved in the diffusion of any technology?

How does gender affect the diffusion of technology? How far do you think these effects are global and how far particular to the developing countries?

The section 'Improved wood-burning stoves' contains a discussion of the technical aims of improving the design and performance of stoves, by eliminating inefficiencies. Summarize this technical material in your own words.

In the same section Agarwal describes why it is so hard to set up a standard testing procedure to measure the efficiency of a stove. She compares an experimental 'boiling water' test with a real-life 'cooking a meal' test. This is an extremely good example of why controlled scientific experiments often give very limited information about the behaviour of the same things being observed outside the laboratory situation. Make notes on Agarwal's criticisms.

What were the measures of success for Sarin's case study? How did the participative process she set up contribute to this success? Can you see the scope for similar participative involvement in design and construction for technological countries?

It is useful to distinguish between *invention* – something new/original often patented, *innovation* – a development/improvement on something which if technically original can also be patented, and *diffusion* or *dissemination* – how the invention/innovation or new idea becomes accessible to as many people as possible.

The issue of low technology stove development is one of 'innovation'; it is an ongoing process as described by Agarwal: Sarin supervised the building of more efficient stoves but the women who were end-users modified and improved the design to optimize it for their own circumstances.

The gender factors involved in the diffusion of innovations apply not only in non-industrialized countries. Remember the discussion about domestic technology in Wajcman: who uses which new tools and equipment – such as videos.

The problem Agarwal identifies of lack of dialogue between 'experts' and 'users' is perhaps worse in industrialized countries where the science and technology are more complex and surrounded with an air of mystery. The chance of being involved in the final product, for example modifying your cooking apparatus, is more difficult although it is possible for artefacts to be designed so that they have a certain amount of flexibility with respect to the needs of the end-user. We have a gendered system in which 'experts' are professionals who are paid to know best. Unfortunately 'experts' have historically been male and 'expertise' an aspect of masculinity, whereas women have been expected to be more literally 'A *Jill* of all trades and a *Master* of none'.

Health risks

The health and safety risks of domestic environments can be at least as dangerous as working environments, and the pollutant effects of low technology can be more severe on individuals than those of high tech.

> Emissions from biomass fuels are dangerous sources of air pollution in the home, where women cook during all or part of the year ... Wood fuels are capable of producing pollution concentrations higher than fossil fuels under slow-burning conditions and some studies have shown that cooks suffer from more smoke and pollutants than residents of the dirtiest urban environments. They are affected by a higher dose than is acceptable under the World Health Organization's recommended level or any national public standard ... In one study quoted by the World Health Organization, a female cook can inhale an amount of benzopyrene (a poisonous gas from burning fuel) equivalent to 20 packs of cigarettes a day. In a few places chronic carbon monoxide poisoning is also evident ...
>
> It seems likely that respiratory and eye diseases, which are so abundant among Third World women and children, are caused by wood and other biomass burning. Exposure can bring acute bronchitis, pneumonia and death where respiratory defences are impaired. Studies also show that where emissions contain high concentrations of carcinogogens, nasopharyngeal cancer is common among young people who have been exposed since infancy.

(Dankelman and Davidson, 1988, p. 72)

4.4 CONSUMPTION AND INFORMATION TECHNOLOGY

Article 4.1 briefly discussed the gendering of some aspects of new technology when they enter homes, in particular video-cassette players and the telephone. Although Agarwal's piece reminds us that we should never take for granted basic physical services, we should also understand the impact of new technology on the domestic environment of developed countries.

Personal computers are the things which immediately spring to mind when we think of new or information technology, but they are only the most obvious aspect. Information technology in the form of microprocessor chips is now designed into the control mechanisms of a variety of artefacts such as dishwashers and washing machines; and other developments in information storage and transmission, such as satellite television and compact discs, also have domestic uses. Many people in the 1980s predicted a social revolution due to the impact of these technologies, but very few feminists were among them.

Feminist analysis had a much clearer sense of the intractability of social relations in general and gender relations in particular. This was likely to lead to a pessimistic position that the impact of new, male-designed and capitalist-produced technologies could only make things worse for women. In the 1990s it appears that both the optimists and pessimists overreacted, and that the impact of new technologies on people's domestic lives has been much less dramatic than predicted by either camp. Despite enthusiastic claims, a computer revolution in the home in particular has failed to materialize.

▶ **ACTIVITY 32** ◀

The following chart is taken from *The Guardian* newspaper and shows the increase in ownership of particular consumer durables in the UK between 1985 and 1990. In order to get you to spend time reading the graph, we have reprinted the text that went with it but with some figures missing. You will need to fill in the missing spaces from your reading of the graph to understand the diffusion of these artefacts into UK homes.

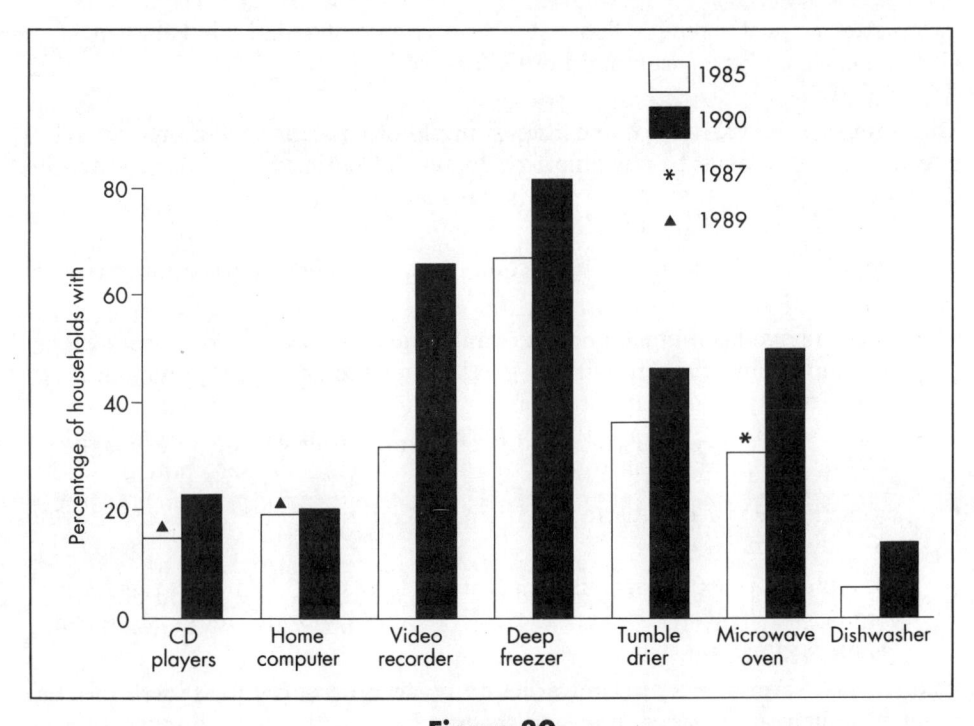

Figure 30
Consumer durables per household, 1985 and 1990
(Note: 1990 data are *provisional* results of the 1990 General Household Survey.)

Compact disc players head list of fastest-growing consumer durables

One in two homes has a microwave cooker and almost two in — have a video recorder, the General Household Survey shows, *writes David Brindle*.

Only 18 per cent of households had videos in 1983, when the survey first counted them, but this had climbed to — per cent in 1990. Microwaves were first counted in 1987 when — per cent had them, but by 1990 they were in — per cent of homes.

The survey has counted consumer durables since 1972, when 42 per cent of homes had a telephone (88 per cent in in 1990), 37 per cent had central heating (80 per cent), 66 per cent had a washing machine (87 per cent), and 52 per cent had a car or a van (67 per cent).

The fastest-growing items in the list at present are microwaves, videos, and especially compact disc players, the last being in — per cent of homes in 1989.

The 1990 count found computers (but excluding video games) in — per cent of homes, television sets in — per cent, tumble driers in — per cent, and dishwashers in — per cent.

(The Guardian, *20 September 1991*)

(The missing information is at the end of this Study Guide.)

What this survey does not indicate is who uses any of these high technology artefacts, and whose labour – if anyone's – they replace or enhance, but feminist research so far suggests that gender will be a determinant of the answers to these questions.

Article 4.4 'The social construction of computers: hammers or harpsichords?' by Gill Kirkup

Read the first three sections of Article 4.4 to the end of 'Personal computers: toys for men and boys?' (pp. 267–73).

The computer provides an interesting example of conflicts in feminist analysis over a particular aspect of technology. In the introductory section the article describes the statistical evidence of women's lack of involvement.

Feminists have argued that:

- women have been involved in computing but their contribution credited to men
- women have been denied a significant contribution to the development of computing by the structured gender inequality in employment and education
- women have been discouraged from computing because it has been gendered in its design
- women have been discouraged from computing because of a *false* masculine image
- computers embody particular masculine forms of logic and these don't come easily to women (there are both feminist and anti-feminist versions of this argument).

Some of these arguments are contradictory but it is certainly possible to hold a number of them at the same time, and the first part of Article 4.4 discusses them in greater detail.

Now read the sections entitled 'IT and women's work' and 'Computing in the education system' (pp. 273–6).

This looks at the predictions of the optimists and pessimists for the impact of IT on women's work. Make sure that you can summarize both. IT is the only technology in the last fifty years that has been claimed as having the potential to break down distinctions between public and private. Not, as feminists suggested, by moving 'privatized' activities like cooking and childcare out to communal facilities but by moving employment, schooling and other activities into the home: the 'electronic cottage'. A few experiments with home IT working attracted much media publicity, but by the early 1990s they have not developed or expanded into significant forms of work.

Now read the final section, 'A machine to think differently with', and the Conclusion (pp. 276–81).

Can you relate Turkle's critique of computing culture to other critiques you have read in Book Three?

Computers are tools to extend our ability to process information – to think, and then raise questions about the nature of thinking. Feminism has asked 'do women think differently from men?', and the answers reflect particular positions. Turkle's critique is similar to that of Fox Keller on the practice of science. They are both postulating not so much that women have a special, better way of doing science/computing, but that science/computing is limited and biased because styles preferred by women (and some men) have been excluded. There are echoes of what Turkle calls bricolage in Fox Keller's description of Barbara McClintock.

4.5 ECOFEMINISM

Ecofeminism can be seen as an extension of the critique of modern science as a masculine project. Ecological problems which result from development and industrialization are identified by writers such as Vandana Shiva as being a direct, even an inevitable, result of masculine science, and the counter to them is seen as lying with women and the non-industrialized poor:

> The parochial roots of science in patriarchy and in a particular class and culture have been concealed behind a claim to universality, and can be seen only through other traditions – of women and non-western peoples. It is these subjugated traditions that are revealing how modern science is gendered, how it is specific to the needs and impulses of the dominant western culture and how ecological destruction and nature's exploitation are inherent in its logic. It is becoming increasingly clear that scientific neutrality has been a reflection of ideology, not history, and science is similar to all other socially constructed categories. This view of science as a social and political project of modern western man is emerging from the responses of those who were defined into nature and made passive and powerless: Mother Earth, women and colonized cultures.
>
> *(Shiva, 1989, p. 21)*

For ecofeminsts such as Shiva and Cat Cox (Article 4.5), there *are* essential connections between women and nature. Western feminism, especially those strands based in forms of materialist philosophy have argued that these connections have been socially constructed to the detriment of women and so should be deconstructed. Ecofeminists argue that this denial of connection is the reason for both the ecological problems we now face as well as for the oppressive nature of patriarchal society. They are pessimists with respect to the potential of modern science and technology regarding them as the physical causes of imminent ecological apocalypse.

Ecofeminism also differs from more mainstream forms of feminism in arguing that this connection between women and nature in particular and humanity and the natural world in general is a spiritual one at least as much as it is a practical one. Feminism in the West has been identified with secular philosophy, and this has been especially so in the second wave when feminism has elaborated concepts taken from liberal humanist philosophy, Marxism and psychoanalysis. Western theology and religion have been identified as sources of oppressive ideology for women; this has meant that some feminists interested in spirituality have redeveloped notions of an Earth Mother or Goddess. (This is discussed further in Radio 04.) This spirituality has underpinned some of the most active episodes of feminist political activism such as Greenham Common. This was captured in the Greenham song which became popular among feminists and Open University Women's Studies students at Summer School:

> You can't kill the Spirit
> She is like a mountain
> Old and strong
> She lives on and on.

It may seem ironic that the part of this course where there is any significant mention of feminist spirituality is in a part dealing with science and technology, but, historically, modern science and religion have been in conflict about the nature of the essence of reality and the ethical systems and behaviour based on that understanding. Ecofeminism is one vision of an essential reality, and of the political activity that should stem from it.

> Now read Article 4.5, 'Ecofeminism'. You will recognize that there are some essentialist arguments underlying Cox's discussion of the connection between women and nature, but she uses other arguments too. As you read, list the arguments she makes, and identify the essentialist ones.

Cox's article gives a summary of some of the most important ecological campaigns mounted by women in both the developed and underdeveloped world. Note that not all of them have been consciously feminist, for example the Chipko Movement. It is not surprising that conscious feminist identification is most common in the West. Cox also gives brief summaries of the most important feminist writings on ecology. Of these perhaps the two most important are Mary Daly's *Gyn/Ecology* (1978) and Susan Griffin's *Women and Nature* (1978); both were controversial when they were first published and remain so because they are stylistically difficult and also because their essentialist and spiritualist tone has been counter to mainstream feminist ideas. However, it should be noted that a group such as the Women's Environmental Network, which at its most prosaic is a consumer action group, does not demand any common philosophy from its members or for its very practical campaigns.

Figure 31
Examples of campaigning leaflets produced by WEN

5
CONCLUSION: SCIENCE, TECHNOLOGY AND IMAGINING THE FUTURE

In the book *Inventing Women* and in the Study Guide material we have tried to show both feminist criticism of the theories and practices of science and technology and the common aims of feminism, science and technology. All three are future directed, and thinking towards the future is a major theme of Chapter 4. Article 4.4, for example, argued optimistically that developments in information technology and feminism could offer alternative styles of thinking and problem-solving. Article 4.5, on the other hand, is pessimistic about developments in science and technology and offers ecofeminism as a philosophy of resistance. Although the essentialism of ecofeminism takes it out of the mainstream of much feminist theory, its general anti-science/anti-technology position is common to much feminism from the last twenty years. But it is certainly *not* our view that this is the inevitable outcome of all feminist critiques of science and technology. The final piece in Book Three, 'Sultana's dream', reflects a time at the beginning of the twentieth century when politically revolutionary ideas and a belief in the liberatory potential of science were not necessarily contradictory. Rokeya Hossain's fiction is interesting because of the cultural and historical period from which it comes, and because since its publication feminist and modernist Utopias have been generally anti-technology. We have chosen to conclude with a piece of fiction that will give you the opportunity to reflect imaginatively on some of the themes in Book Three as well as a way of providing a link with your later work in Book Four, *Imagining Women*.

> Now read Hossain's story, 'Sultana's dream'. Note what for her are the most crucial aspects of living for which she finds technological solutions. Relate these to some of the articles you have read earlier in Book Three. Does she have what you feel is a consistent view of gender difference or feminist values, and who in her story embodies these?

For Hossain there are technological solutions to the provision of energy and water. These solve the problem of agricultural labour, domestic labour and transport, which leave women free to administer justice and pursue leisure activities such as embroidery. Article 4.2 demonstrates why technical solutions to cooking and the provision of water were and are so important to an Indian feminist. Her belief in the power of education in a country where few women were educated is reflected in the concerns of present-day feminist educators in non-industrialized countries (see, for example, Article 3.2). The feminist society she envisions is peaceful but not pacifist and she imagines the use of high energy weaponry designed and directed by women against an enemy, but there is no death penalty in the justice system. The women in the society are credited with being essentially more rational than the men who 'are capable of doing no end of mischief' and who are compared with lunatics and wild animals. The Queen is the embodiment of these feminist values and the revolution is credited to her vision, and especially to her belief in education. Hossain's vision of gender difference is not consistent: for example, men are seen as dangerous and too impatient to do embroidery but they are given the children to take care of. The society of Ladyland is as sex-segregated as traditional Indian society, but the secluded sex is now male. There is no vision of gender equality or of a gender-neutral science. In Ladyland the sexes are seen as the obverse of each other, with the possibility of only one holding power. Although this is sometimes still a solution or scenario for feminist science fiction, it appeals less to modern feminist thinking than solutions which look for the dissemination of 'female' attributes and feminist values into all society and into the practice of science.

ANSWERS TO ACTIVITIES

Activity 2

We hope you had no problem interpreting these data; none of the tables that you will find scattered throughout this Study Guide will be any more difficult than this.

(a) Men were 7 per cent of students registered on this course. Did it surprise you? Many women wonder why any men at all do a women's studies course, while men on the course often wonder why more men don't do it.

(b) The largest occupational category amongst this group was housewives: full time and part-time together accounted for one third of all the students.

(c) The largest paid occupational group were clerical workers (16 per cent).

(d) Only 3 per cent of women students were qualified scientists or engineers or technical personnel.

(e) The ratio of these to clerical workers is 3:16 or roughly one to five.

(f) There are some obvious problems with the data we have given you: you cannot separate the men from the women in terms of their occupations, and you would expect there to be a difference. You also have no idea what kind of occupational category those women are in who have classified themselves as housewives in part-time work, or how much work you have to do before you classify yourself as in an occupation other than housewife. The categories also do not allow men to be 'househusbands', nor for them to be part-time workers.

(g) Finally, the largest proportion (61 per cent) of students had studied a foundation course in the Arts faculty; 57 per cent had studied Social Sciences (D courses), while Technology, Mathematics and Science had each been studied by 5 per cent or fewer of the total group.

Activity 3

(a) Arts has the largest number of women students: 35,900 on first degree courses (full-time and part-time); and 48,000 in total. The smallest number are in applied science: 7,000 women in total.

(b) Pure science has the largest number of men: 41,200 first degree students (full-time and part-time); 55,900 men in total. Arts has the smallest number: 20,900 first degree students and 35,200 in total.

(c) 30,700 women were studying pure science compared with 7,000 studying applied science: this is a ratio of roughly 1:4.

(d) The total number of women on first degree courses (full-time and part-time) was 89,000, compared with 124,900 men: a ratio of roughly 5:7.

(e) 25.6 per cent of all men students are studying applied science but only 6.2 per cent of women.

(f) Proportions going on to study at postgraduate level are as follows:

Arts	68.4% of men	33.7% of women
Social Science	48.6	30.3
Applied Science	33.7	28.6
Pure Science	35.7	23.3

Activity 18

Prenatal screening techniques

Screening techniques	Used to detect	Disadvantages
AFB blood test (from mother)	neural tube defects	if in doubt must be followed by further tests, e.g. amniocentesis – sometimes done without mother's permission
amniocentesis (taking amniotic fluid)	primarily: Down's syndrome and chromosome abnormalities but also neural tube defects and sex	• late stage of pregnancy • long lab. process • risk of miscarriage
Foetoscopy	primarily metabolic problems	risk of miscarriage
CVS – via cervix or abdomen – foetal cells direct	genetic diseases where more cells are needed for detection	• cannot diagnose neural tube defects • less reliable than amniocentesis • risk of miscarriage
ultrasound (by itself)	• major congenital defects • sex • number of foetuses • used to guide amniocentis and CVS tests	unreliable at early stages of pregnancy

Activity 22

	CSE		O-level		A-level	
	Boys	Girls	Boys	Girls	Boys	Girls
% increase 1968–82	220	1150	66	192	28	100

(Your answer may vary slightly depending on how you interpreted the values on the graph.)

CSE Girls entries in 1968   2,000   entries in 1983   25,000
Actual increase in numbers between 1968 and 1983 = 23,000

$$\% \text{ increase} = \frac{23\,000}{2\,000} \times 100$$
$$= 1150\%$$

In each case the percentage increase in the number of girls entering is much greater than that of boys.

ANSWERS TO ACTIVITIES

Activity 24

Occupation	Female as % of total	As % of total women
Managerial staff	5.1	1.7
Professional engineers, scientists and technologists	5.2	1.2
Technicians and technician engineers, including draughtsmen	3.5	1.5
Administrative and professional staff	21	7.1
Clerks, office machine operators, secretaries and typist	76	34.2
Supervisors	9.3	2.1
Craftsmen in occupations normally entered by apprenticeship	0.9	0.8
Operators and other employees (excluding canteen staff)	25	51.4
Overall	20.5	100

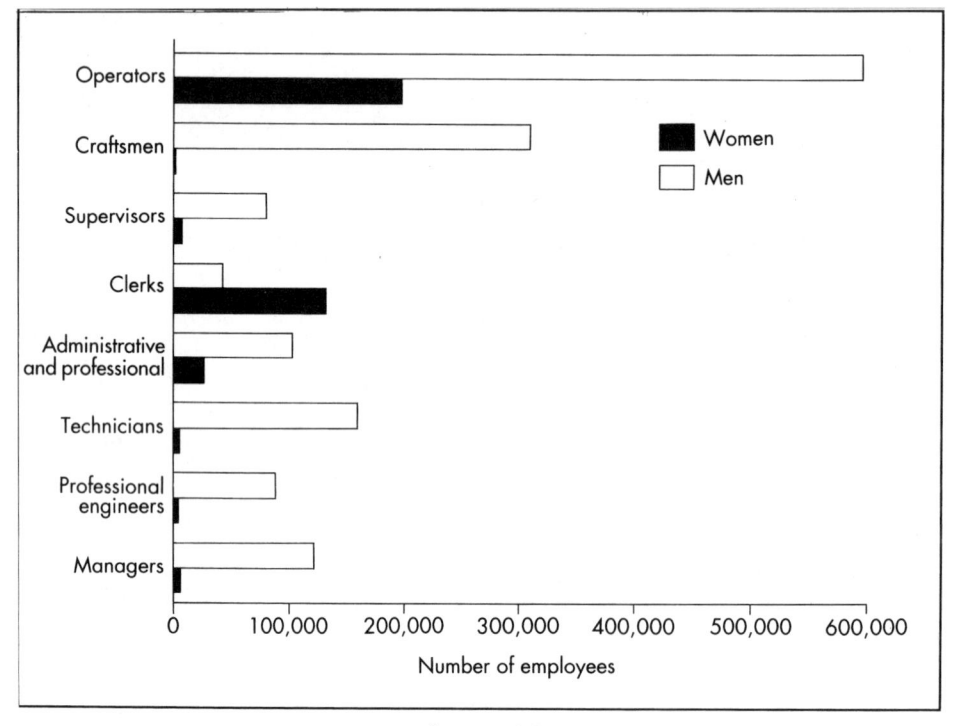

Figure 32
British Engineering Industry: estimated number of employees, analysed by occupational category and sex, April 1989

Activity 32

- two in three have a video recorder
- 64 per cent had videos in 1990
- microwaves grew from 30 per cent to 50 per cent
- compact disc players grew from 15 to 21 per cent
- computers 20 per cent
- televisions 98 per cent
- freezers 81 per cent
- tumble driers 46 per cent
- dishwashers 12 per cent.

OBJECTIVES

The following is a list of the objectives of this part of the course. These are the things that you should be able to do when you have completed your study of Book Three and this Study Guide. They have been listed here for revision purposes with articles from Book Three that are especially relevant noted beside each one, as well as the numbers of activities where you were dealing with particular ideas or skills

▶ SUGGESTED REVISION EXERCISE FOR THE END OF ◀ THE COURSE

Read through each objective assessing yourself according to whether you feel *very confident* that you can do it (grade it 3), *reasonably confident* (grade it 2) or *not very confident* (grade it 1). Then take all those which you have graded '1' and refer back to the readings, activities and your notes and spend more of your revision time on those than the others.

Compare these objectives with those in other Study Guides (they may have been presented differently), look for common themes and concepts. If you have time you could try writing each objective from each Study Guide on a separate piece of paper, then sorting them into piles with common themes regardless of which Study Guide they came from. You might find that doing this helps you to stop thinking of the objectives as tightly tied to any one part of the course, and that connecting themes emerge more clearly than you had previously been aware. If you spent some time on an activity like this you could completely redesign the course by reorganizing the content into a differently structured sequence!

1. Give a definition of modern science, describe its historical context. and the way in which a particular set of methods has come to dominate Western thought. (Articles Intro 1, 1.1, 1.3, 1.4, 3.3, 4.5; SG Activities 4, 7)

2. Compare different feminist criticisms of the practice of science (Articles 1.3, 1.4, 2.1, 2.2, 3.3, 4.5)

3. Describe the biological and anthropological evidence for sex differences and discuss the meaning of this data with respect to the social organization of men and women. (2.1, 2.2, 2.3; SG Activities 8, 9, 10)

4. Discuss the concept of reproductive rights and give examples of the technologies associated with it. (2.3, 2.4; Activities 16, 17, 18)

5. Discuss medical technology as a crucial area of struggle for women, over power and rights (giving examples). (2.3, 2.4; Activities 12, 13, 14, 15, 16)

6. Illustrate the way race, class and geographical location combine with gender to produce unequal access to science and technology and to its products. (1.1, 1.2, 2.3, 2.4, 3.4, 3.7, 4.2; Activities 6, 14, 15)

7. Discuss the scientific and technological professions as examples of professions where male power has been used to exclude women, and give examples. (3.1, 3.2, 3.4, 3.6; Activity 19)

8. Discuss how technical skills have historically been equated with masculinity and give examples of how these are structured into

training and employment in ways that exclude women. (3.2, 3.4, 3.6; Activity 24, 25, 32)

9   Discuss how both the curriculum and teaching practices have operated to discriminate against girls in science education. (3.2; Activities 3, 22, 23)

10 Discuss how artefacts become gendered in their design and production, and give examples. (3.6, 4.1, 4.4; Activity 28)

11 List the different stages in the process of the development and dissemination of science and technology, such as design, production, transfer, diffusion, and discuss how gender is significant at each stage. (3.7, 4.2)

12 Compare the impact of developments in domestic technology on women in developed and underdeveloped countries, and discuss this as an example of the power of social and economic factors over technical developments. (4.2; Activities 29, 30, 31)

13 Discuss how the design of the domestic environment (the workplace of most women) is controlled by ideology about family life, class and the role of women. Illustrate this by an analysis of real space as well as textual examples. (4.1; Activities 27, 28, 29)

14 Describe the interrelationship between militarism and masculinity and the impact this has had on developments in technology, and social gender divisions. (3.6, 4.4; Activities 10, 26)

15 Speculate about the impact on women of developments in information technology, based on the evidence of impacts so far. (4.4; Activity 32)

16 Interpret and evaluate statistical information presented in the form of tables, graphs and charts. (Activities 2, 3, 5, 15, 22, 23, 24, 25, 26, 31, 32)

17 Critically evaluate biographies in terms of style and argument. (Article 3.3; Activities 20, 21)

REFERENCES

ABU-LUGHOD, L. (1991) 'Can there be a feminist ethnography?', *Women & Performance: A Journal of Feminist Theory*, Vol.5, No. 1, Issue 9, pp. 7-27.

AQUINAS, T. (1267–73) *Summa Theologica*, quoted in O'Faolain, J. and Martines, L. (1979) *Not in God's Image*, London, Virago Press.

BARASH, D. (1980) *Sociobiology: the whisperings within*, London, Souvenir Press.

BERER, M. (1988) 'Whatever happened to "A Woman's Right to Choose"?', *Feminist Review*, No. 29, Spring.

BLUE, A. (1987) *Grace under Pressure*, London, Sidgewick and Jackson.

BOSTON WOMEN'S HEALTH BOOK COLLECTIVE (1976) *Our Bodies, Our Selves*, New York, Simon and Schuster.

COCKBURN, C. (1985) *Machinery of Dominance: women, men and technical know-how*, London, Pluto Press.

DALY, M. (1978) *Gyn/Ecology: the metaethics of radical feminism*, Boston, MA, Beacon Press.

DANKELMAN, I. and DAVIDSON, J. (1988) *Women and Environment in the Third World: alliance for the future*, London, Earthscan.

DAVIES, M. LLEWELYN (ed.) (1914) *Maternity: Letters from Working Women, Collected by the Women's Co-operative Guild* (new edn, London, Virago Press, 1978).

GILLIGAN, C. (1982) *In a Different Voice: psychological theory and women's development*, Cambridge, MA, Harvard University Press.

GRIFFIN, S. (1984) *Woman and Nature*, London, The Women's Press.

HARDING, S. (1986) *The Science Question in Feminism*, Milton Keynes, Open University Press.

HOME OFFICE (1975) *A Guide to the Sex Discrimination Act 1975*, London, HMSO.

KANE, P. (1991) *Women's Health: from womb to tomb*, Basingstoke and London, Macmillan.

KUHN, T.S. (1962) *The Structure of Scientific Revolutions*, Chicago, Chicago University Press.

MORRIS, D. (1967) *The Naked Ape: a zoologist's study of the human animal*, London, Jonathan Cape.

MUELLER, L. (1983) 'A Nude by Edward Hopper' from Raving Beauties (eds) *In the Pink*, London, The Women's Press.

SEAGER, J. and OLSON. A. (1986) *Women in the World: an international atlas*, London, Pluto Press.

TOMASELLI, (1991) 'Science as culture', *Feminist Review*, No. 40, pp. 95–106.

VARE, E.A. and PTACEK, G. (1987) *Mothers of Invention – from the Bra to the Bomb: forgotten women and their unforgettable ideas*, New York, Quill, William Morrow.

WHEELWRIGHT, J. (1989) *Amazons and Military Maids: women who dressed as men in pursuit of life, liberty and happiness*, London, Pandora Press.

ACKNOWLEDGEMENTS

Grateful acknowledgement is made to the following sources for permission to reproduce material in this Study Guide:

Text

p. 22: Lisel Mueller for 'A Nude by Edward Hopper', published in *Rising Tides*, Washington Square Press, c/o Simon & Schuster, New York; *pp. 52–4:* Vare E.A. and Ptacek, G., *Mothers of Invention – From the Bra to the Bomb: forgotten women and their unforgettable ideas*, 1987, Quill/William Morrow, New York; *pp. 91–2*: Brindle D. 'Compact disc players head list of fastest growing consumer durables', *The Guardian*, 20 September 1991.

Figures

Figure 1: John Driscoll for 'Cheat slur costs job', *Times Higher Education Supplement*, 6 September 1991, cartoon by Andrew Birch, reproduced by permission of the artist; *Figure 2*: facsimile-typogravure of Mary Cassatt's decoration, reproduced by courtesy of Chicago Historical Society; *Figure 3*: *Women and Men in Britain*, 1987, Equal Opportunities Commission, reproduced with the permission of the Controller of Her Majesty's Stationery Office; *Figure 4*: Associated Press; *Figure 5*: Ancient Art and Architecture Collection; *Figure 6*: Mansell Collection; *Figure 7*: Durham, Michael, 'Ministers make U-turn on breast cancer testing', cartoon by Newman, *The Sunday Times*, 29 September 1991, both © Times Newspapers Ltd 1991; *Figure 8*: Advertising Archives, London; *Figure 9*: John Driscoll for 'Campus grapples with carnage aftermath', *Times Higher Education Supplement*, 15 September 1989; *Figure 10*: Associated Press; *Figure 11*: Archiv zur Geschichte der Max-Planck-Gesellschaft, Berlin (Mappe XI.17.Nr 3, Q16-1-14); *p. 55*: cartoon by Bill Tidy, *New Scientist*, 14 September 1991, reproduced by permission of the artist; *Figure 13*: Figures 20 and 21 of EHP532 *Primary Science: case studies in learning and assessment, The Assessment Book*, 1991, Milton Keynes, The Open University; *Figure 14*: 'New exams would hold back girls', *Architects Journal*, 6 November 1991, p. 7, Architectural Press; *Figure 15*: from 'Degrees of difference', *The Observer*, 24 February 1991, © The Observer 1991; *Figure 16*: *Women and Men in Britain*, 1991, Equal Opportunities Commission, reproduced with the permission of the Controller of Her Majesty's Stationery Office; *Figure 17*: Associated Press; *Figure 18*: Reproduced by courtesy of the Information Counsellor's Office of the Turkish Embassy, London; *Figure 19*: Photo: B.Pratt/Oxfam; *Figures 20–26*: Matrix (eds), *Making Space: women and the man-made environment*, 1984, London, Pluto Press, by permission of the publishers; *Figures 28 and 29*: Advertising Archives, London; *Figure 30*: data from OPCS Monitor 'General Household Survey, Preliminary results for 1990', Series SS 91/1, © Crown Copyright; *p. 93*: *New Internationalist*, July 1991; *Figure 31*: Women's Environmental Network leaflets – Campaign for Minimum Packaging and Campaign for Unbleached Packaging, reproduced by permission of the artist, Angela Martin, page one of Women's Environmental Network Newsletter, No. 9, Winter 1990, by courtesy of Women's Environmental Network.

Tables

Table 3: Kane P., *Womens' Health: from womb to tomb*, 1991, Macmillan Publishers Ltd; *Table 4*: Boston Women's Health Collective, *Our Bodies, Our Selves*, 1971, Simon & Schuster, New York; *Table 5*: The Association for Women in Science, Washington, DC; *Table 7*: Agarwal B., *Cold Hearths and Barren Slopes*, 1986, Zed Books.